hairspray

The Roots

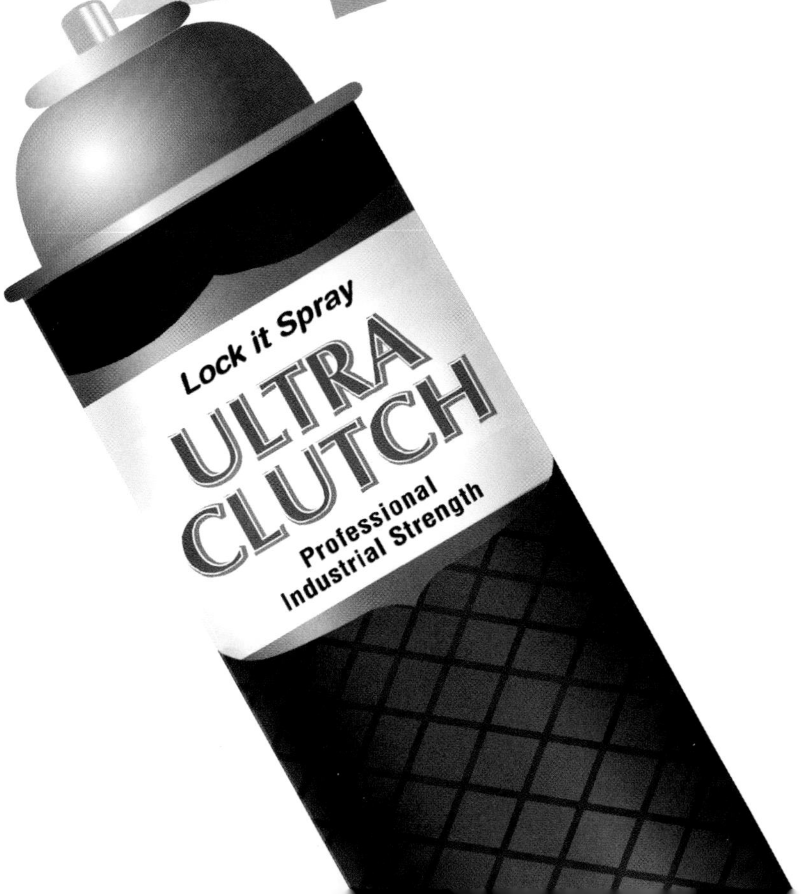

ULTRA CLUTCH

hair

A Roundtable Press Book

Hosted by the Authors of
the Hit Broadway Musical

MARK O'DONNELL

THOMAS MEEHAN

MARC SHAIMAN

SCOTT WITTMAN

spray

The Roots

Interview with **JOHN WATERS**
and **MARGO LION** by **J. WYNN ROUSUCK**

FABER AND FABER, INC.
An affiliate of Farrar, Straus and Giroux

Principal Photography by **PAUL KOLNIK**

A Roundtable Press Book

ff

FABER AND FABER, INC.
An affiliate of Farrar, Straus and Giroux
19 Union Square West, New York 10003

Distributed in Canada by Penguin Books of
    Canada Limited
Printed in the United States of America
First edition, 2003

ALL PHOTOGRAPHS © 2002 PAUL KOLNIK, EXCEPT:

Pages 4, 14, 16 (bottom), 43 (top), 44 (left), 64-69
    (backgrounds), 84, 92 (bottom, second from right),
    92 (bottom, far right), 126-131 (backgrounds), 167
    (far right): © 2002 Eric Laignel/Rockwell Group
Page 6: J. Wynn Rousuck
Page 15 (upper left): Colleen Croft

Pages 17 (lower right), 29 (lower left), 35 (lower right),
    47 (top right), 47 (middle right), 47 (lower right),
    47 (bottom right), 58 (top left), 76 (top left), 76
    (middle left), 89 (bottom right), 96 (top), 127 (lower
    left), 128 (top right), 128 (top left), 129 (center),
    133 (small spot), 152 (middle right): Photofest
Pages 25 (top right), 92 (bottom, far left), 92 (bottom,
    second from left), 93 (top), 93 (top right), 93
    (bottom center), 93 (bottom right), 106-107 (center):
    © 2002 Rockwell Group
Page 33 (lower left): JFK Library
Page 78 (top right): Donald Sanders
Page 92 (top right): Jim Franco
Page 166 (opening night curtain, center): Tracey Berg
Page 166 (opening night curtain, bottom): Richard Read
Page 167 (top right): Walter McBride/Retna Ltd. USA
Page 168: Anne Marino

A mother lode of thanks to Harvey Fierstein for
contributing a mother load of marvelous imagery to this
book. Photographs appearing on the following pages
©2002 Harvey Fierstein: 20 (middle right), 21 (top row,
second from left), 21 (second row, second from right),
21 (bottom right), 36 (all), 37 (all), 38 (top right).

Special thanks to Linda Hart for her "soup-to-nuts"
behind-the-scenes camera work. Photographs appearing
on the following pages © 2002 Linda Hart: 5 (bottom
left), 20 (top left), 20 (middle, far left), 20 (middle,

second from left), 20 (bottom, far left), 20 (bottom, far
right), 21 (top, second from right), 29 (top right), 39,
71 (bottom right), 167 (center).

Drawings on pages 78, 79, 144, and 145 courtesy
William Ivey Long

After party invitation on page 166 designed by
Peter Koblish

Show logo courtesy of Serino Coyne, Inc.
Front cover photograph: Norman Jean Roy
Back cover photograph: Eric Laignel/Rockwell Group

Special thanks to Actors Equity Association and the cast
and crew of *Hairspray*.

For Roundtable Press, Inc.
DIRECTORS: Julie Merberg and Marsha Melnick
EXECUTIVE EDITOR: Patty Brown
EDITOR: John Glenn
ASSOCIATE EDITOR: Sara Newberry
DESIGN: Georgia Rucker, www.pinkdesigninc.com
PRODUCTION: Bill Rose

Library of Congress Control Number: 2003100750

ISBN 0-571-21143-7
www.fsgbooks.com

10 9 8 7 6 5 4 3 2 1

Preface

A QUICK WASH BEFORE STYLING

There's a classic old *New Yorker* cartoon in which a woman at a beauty parlor is told, "You're one of the lucky few who have *normal* hair." The fact is, very few of us, in our success-addled culture, ever feel we have normal-enough hair, or are truly and completely normal, anyway, and that may be where the appeal of *Hairspray* kicks in. Tenacious Tracy Turnblad, lovable as she is, is fat, and all of us, lovable as we are, are somehow, metaphorically, fat. Skinny, clumsy, new in town, female, foreign, black, Jewish, gay, naive, brainy, too short, too tall, overeager, shy, poor, left-handed, over-freckled, pyrokinetic (like *Carrie*), scissor-handed (like *Edward*), or musical-comedy–loving—there's always something real or imagined that keeps the individual apart from the tantalizing but narrow-minded In Crowd. *Hairspray* is about acceptance and inclusiveness, and the child (or worse, the teen) in everyone can identify with the longing to belong. It's supposed to be We the People, after all.

A Mount Rushmore of moxie: song-writers Marc Shaiman and Scott Wittman flank stars Harvey Fierstein and Marissa Winokur.

The team that assembled *Hairspray* certainly had Tracy-like adolescences. John Waters, the founder of this feast, has come to epitomize how to take outsider status and make it work for you. All of us were show-biz fans from an early age, hying mostly from the hinterlands, and writing for Broadway was a dream each of us nurtured (sometimes secretly, to avoid getting beaten up), just the way Tracy dreams of getting on Corny Collins's show. The slightly foolish ecstasy she experiences when she gets on TV is no less than the selfish-yet-joint joy we all felt when the roses and flashbulbs swirled around us on opening night. Sally Field can vouch for how nice it is to be liked. Willy Loman ("He's liked, but he's not *well liked*"), Shylock, and Othello might have had more fun if they'd had the good luck to star in comedies instead of tragedies. Nonetheless, when we began our "Cinderella for Cynics," we figured as long as we were tailor-making a wish-fulfillment with a social message, we'd be most effective if we soft-pedaled the Message part and tried to make the proceedings kinetic, funny, and a little unexpectedly rude. For credibility's sake, a spoonful of acid helps the happiness go down.

Book writers Tom Meehan and Mark O'Donnell demonstrate that shtick in the theater isn't limited to the actors.

Affable assistant director Matt Lenz (left) and the creative team watch a rehearsal in a studio space high above fabled 42nd Street.

Mark and Tom in a huddle with head coach and fearless leader Jack O'Brien.

Mark O'Donnell

Thomas Meehan

Marc Shaiman

Scott Wittman

A Conversation with John Waters and Margo Lion

J. Wynn Rousuck, Theater Critic, The Baltimore Sun

August 15, 2002, was a very, very, very good hair day for John Waters and Margo Lion. Not just good, but big, boffo, bouffant—and that's no tease. August 15 was the day *Hairspray* opened on Broadway to rave reviews, quickly becoming New York's latest musical megahit.

Lion is *Hairspray*'s originating producer. It was her idea to make a musical of Waters's 1988 movie—the story of a tubby, blue-collar, socially conscious Baltimore teen named Tracy Turnblad, who wins a coveted place on an early 1960s local TV dance show, *The Corny Collins Show*, and bands together with friends and family to break its color barrier.

To adapt the movie to the stage, Lion commissioned a team of writers consisting of composer-lyricist Marc Shaiman, co-lyricist Scott Wittman, and book writers Mark O'Donnell and Thomas Meehan. She also enlisted a team of experienced co-producers. Together they hired Harvey Fierstein to play Tracy's mom (the role created on screen by Divine, Waters's late cross-dressing star) and Marissa Jaret Winokur to play Tracy (the role that launched Ricki Lake's career).

To capture the look of 1960s Baltimore—from row houses with their Formstone™ fronts to towering beehive hairdos—Lion and her partners brought in a design team headed by David Rockwell (sets), William Ivey Long (costumes), Kenneth Posner (lighting), and Paul Huntley (hair).

Waters and Lion discussed the musical's genesis during a long conversation at the filmmaker's New York apartment, a cozy Greenwich Village condo that he describes as "the coolest hotel suite I always wished I had." The walls are painted various shades of his favorite color ("puke green") and display art ranging from a George Stoll sculpture of a toilet-paper holder that dispenses green chiffon to a painting of an asshole by Andy Warhol, which Waters gave himself as a present after making his 2000 movie *Cecil B. Demented*. Nestled on the green velvet sofa is a needlepoint pillow of an electric chair, lovingly stitched by Waters's mother.

The filmmaker and the producer are both from Baltimore, and both were in high school during the era when *Hairspray* takes place. Each day after school, like countless other Baltimore teens, they came home and watched *The Buddy Deane Show*, the local TV program that inspired *Hairspray*. But Waters and Lion never imagined that *Buddy Deane*, Baltimore's answer to *American Bandstand*, would link them in the annals of Broadway history.

As he does for all his guests, Waters began the interview by taking a Polaroid photo of Lion and me. (As the theater critic of the *Baltimore Sun* and, previously, one of its arts reporters, I've covered both their careers for years.) I then turned the camera on Waters, shooting a few Polaroids of him with Lion as they recalled their impressions of one another at their first meeting—a lunch at New York's Orso restaurant in the spring of 1999.

JOHN WATERS: Well, Margo, to me you didn't look like a producer. You didn't look like you were from Baltimore, but I believed everything you said, and I don't know why.

MARGO LION: And I couldn't believe that you were such a gentleman and so easy to talk to.

JW: Well, what did you think I was going to be? A puke eater?

ML: Hmm, just someone who spoke another language. How's that for diplomacy? But you were so courtly.

JW: Portly?

ML: Courtly! Courtly! And after that first meeting I kept thinking about how much fun it was going to be.

JW: Certainly the thing I remember is that you said you really wanted to keep the flavor of a John Waters movie. And I knew that you didn't mean *Pink Flamingos*.

ML: That's for sure. Anyway, it was *your* film that captured my imagination. It was crucial that your personality define the experience; any attempt to ignore your voice would be a cop-out.

JW: (Laughing) Because, basically, if I didn't like it, I could dish it in the press.

ML: I guess you could say it was important to me from a commercial as well as an artistic perspective. Okay?

JW: What I realized was that the play had to become something different from the movie for it to work. It had to cross over into something else.

Lion had offered Waters the chance to write the script for the musical, but he declined.

JW: I think I would have been crazy to do that, and I think the writers did a great job. I was in the middle of writing a movie.

ML: You were amazing at letting us re-imagine the work for the stage—I don't remember you ever being territorial about the material.

JW: But it's not like I didn't say anything.

ML: Right. You were the Bible. If there ever was a question about authenticity, there you were. Your word was law. Remember, "No Goucher (far too upscale). Tracy should go to Essex Community College"?

JW: You hired the right people. A great team. That is so hard to do. Everybody seemed like they had been working together forever.

ML: Let's face it: you were a hero to our writers and they adored you. They wanted you to be happy.

JW: It was an incredible learning experience for me. It was like going to graduate school in theater arts.

* Peter Pingleton announces extended tour of duty, though war is over and he's a civilian.
* Amber Von Tussle is born, a rare "chauffeured" birth.
* *Gentleman's Agreement* gives tolerance a glossy if vague endorsement.

1948
* Tracy's first words are "mama" and "cha-cha."
* Ralph Ellison and Richard Wright have had "just about enough."

1949
* Amber has her first tantrum: her booties not color-coordinated.
* Russia gets A-bomb; world experiences mixed dread and denial from now until 1990.

1950
* Motormouth Maybelle Stubbs is voted hottest established singer in Baltimore; Little Inez is born.
* "Ragg Mopp" (by the Ames Brothers) is the dumbest song to ever top pop charts.

1951
* After trying rocking and rolling separately, music pioneers decide to rock and roll simultaneously.

1952
* Mamie Eisenhower is square even by 1950s standards.
* Velma's husband dies in freak porno parlor explosion; she inherits TV station, fortune.
* Penny is asked to repeat kindergarten after failing lunch.

1953
* Queen Elizabeth is crowned, inspiring Tracy and Amber.
* Russians oppress millions, inspiring Amber.

1954
* Teens rock around the clock, despite nuclear menace, or perhaps because of it.
* Velma discovers that "payola" is not a candy bar.

For Lion, the movie Hairspray *was also a learning experience. She had seen the film when it came out but admits she didn't fully appreciate it. Then she rented the video and watched it while recovering from a cold in early 1999. The video may not have opened her sinuses, but it definitely opened her eyes.*

ML: It had all the ingredients for a successful musical: a larger-than-life character, preferably a heroine, who is forced to overcome obstacles to achieve her dream. And the big bonus was that the material had personality. It felt new, not like a pale imitation of a traditional musical.

JW: Did you realize that when the people who were on *The Buddy Deane Show* first saw the movie, they said they felt as if they were in the Twilight Zone? The movie was authentic. It *wasn't* exaggerated. That *is* how everybody looked.

ML: I used to dance with my pillow while I watched *The Buddy Deane Show*.

JW: Usually kids danced with the refrigerator door or the radiator. The teenagers on *Buddy Deane* called themselves "continental." In East Baltimore that was the fabulous look, but it was thought of as low-class in preppy neighborhoods. So the Committee members [called the Council in the musical] would go from one neighborhood to another and either get beaten up or sign autographs. They didn't know what would happen from their local celebrity. It just depended, literally, which block they were on. But I thought the kids on the show looked great, and obviously even Divine in *Female Trouble* looks like a Buddy Deaner. In the movie, she's a juvenile delinquent with the teased hair and cha-cha heels. It's still one of the most bizarre looks in fashion history. Women wore those hairdos and that makeup *every day*. That's a lot of beauty work. Margo, you didn't have teased hair, even in the early sixties?

ML: Well, just a *little bit* teased.

In May 2000, the first act of Hairspray, *a musical-in-progress, received a reading for an audience of invited guests at the New York Theatre Workshop.*

JW: I went alone, and I was stunned by it. I just sort of sat there thinking how very strange it was, because of Divine. When the movie came out, it was a hit also, and we got all these rave reviews and everything, and then Divine died a week later. So I don't remember the success. The death wiped out all the great feelings I would have had. So the Broadway show being a success meant I could continue the happiness that was stopped back then, because I never got to celebrate except for the first six days after the film was released. Then a funeral. I wanted to cry opening night, "How did this happen fourteen years later?" It's just amazing, but I'm glad I lived to see it.

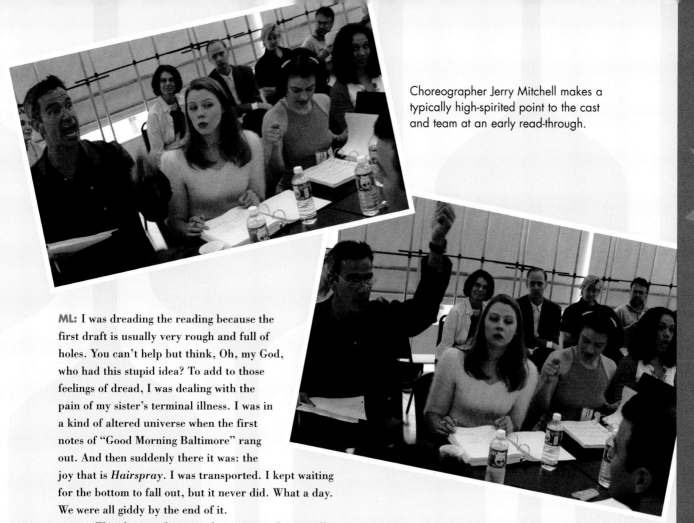

Choreographer Jerry Mitchell makes a typically high-spirited point to the cast and team at an early read-through.

ML: I was dreading the reading because the first draft is usually very rough and full of holes. You can't help but think, Oh, my God, who had this stupid idea? To add to those feelings of dread, I was dealing with the pain of my sister's terminal illness. I was in a kind of altered universe when the first notes of "Good Morning Baltimore" rang out. And then suddenly there it was: the joy that is *Hairspray*. I was transported. I kept waiting for the bottom to fall out, but it never did. What a day. We were all giddy by the end of it.

That first reading was the moment when we all became a team. You were always supportive of the project and not intrusive at all. But you *were* reserved about casting. And when I say "reserved," I don't mean you were critical; you just didn't comment.

JW: It was so hard for me to imagine. These parts were "owned" by these other people. It was hard for me to give up Divine and Ricki and all the people who originated those parts.

ML: Of course.

JW: Marc Shaiman had suggested Harvey Fierstein, and as soon as I heard him do it I thought he was absolutely perfect. But I hadn't seen Harvey in twenty years, so I didn't know. I had known Harvey slightly, a little bit really, a long time ago. I always was a fan of his. I had seen his plays. I even have them as books. And another thing: Harvey's a writer. The fact that Harvey is a writer, has written plays and everything, adds to his performance, adds to his timing, adds to how he works with people. It's a real luxury to have actors who are writers.

ML: How did you feel about Marissa playing Ricki Lake's role?

JW: I knew it would be trickier because Ricki's not only alive—she's quite successful. I'm still very close to her and it was hard, at first, for me to imagine anyone else in the role but I realized this is a Broadway musical, *not* a film remake. Marissa was a Broadway baby right from the start and put her own spin on the role immediately. Amazing to me—I thought up a part that made *two* young actresses famous. When we cast the movie, Ricki Lake was the only *real* candidate and Marissa Jaret Winokur was the Broadway version right from the get-go.

During the movie, Ricki started to lose weight, and I remember we would feed her cupcakes and Dove Bars and stuff. In the very beginning I said to Margo, "Don't make Tracy plump."

ML: You kept saying that to me.

JW: Fat, we want. Not plump.

1961
* Link Larkin is declared most happening guy at Patterson Park High School; administration refuses to acknowledge Link happening.

1962
* Liz leaves Eddie for Dick.
* New fall model cars most breathtaking ever, say publicists.
* Baltimore Eventorium opens.
* Tracy becomes overnight star.
* (YOU ARE HERE.)

1963
* Baltimore Eventorium collapses.
* Velma and Prudy are admitted to clinic for treatment of acute uptightness; Amber is given treatment on outpatient basis.
* Link and Tracy are voted king and queen of prom but then disqualified because of low grade averages.
* Seaweed has more soul than he can control; Penny offsets his excess.

1964
* Beatles bring added sensibility to popular music discourse; teen girls scream.
* Congress passes national Civil Rights Act; South pretends not to notice.
* Nation grows tired of Singing Along with Mitch.
* Tang's popularity marks end of civilized culture.

1965
* Link and Tracy get matching Graduate Equivalency Degrees in solemn ceremony, attend prom "by mail."
* Massive recall of Ultra Clutch cans due to radioactive "cling" molecules; straight hair becomes popular as a result.

1966
* Tracy and Link record "Tummy Full of Love," their first hit as a duo; PTAs nationwide try to figure out if song is obscene.

- Edna's fashion designs sweep the Pinky Awards.
- Spiro Agnew is poised to take his evil nationwide.

1967
- Corny experiments with mustache and sideburns; his show is canceled.
- Seaweed and Penny wed; Prudy dies.
- Amber wins Miss America title in her own deluded mind.

1968
- Nixon is elected; country feels funny (not "funny ha-ha," but "funny peculiar").
- Tracy and Link top charts with "You Know Me, Babe"; parents' groups ask, "In the biblical sense?"

1969
- Tracy and Link make breakthrough "rock 'n' road" movie, *Easygoing Drivers,* and win simultaneous joint Oscar, Grammy, and Emmy awards (the Emmys for their Oscar and Grammy acceptance speeches).
- Man lands on the moon.

1970
- Wilbur opens Har-De-Har Land, amusement park with emphasis on rides that squirt stuff and make embarrassing noises.
- Corny hosts network game show *What's Your Bag?*

1971
- Have a Nice Day craze sweeps America, due to marijuana-addled judgment.
- Link and Tracy win new plaudits for serious roles in telefilm *Franklin and Eleanor: The Big Band Years.*

1972
- Nixon is reelected; joke begins to wear thin.

John Waters, director Jack O'Brien, and star Harvey Fierstein: chief conspirators in the perpetration of *Hairspray.*

Harvey and John: pop icons in conference.

ML: "It's gotta be fat, Margo, it's gotta be fat." I guess you did read my mind because left to my own devices I might have tried to hedge my bets and go "plump." But of course, you were right. You used to call me a "fattist."

JW: You *are* a fattist.

As part of his official role as Hairspray *consultant, Waters took the show's director, Jack O'Brien, choreographer Jerry Mitchell, and set designer David Rockwell on his own distinctive tour of Baltimore in November 2001.*

JW: They all came to my house, and we talked a lot. Then we did my tour, which I've done many times. We went to Highlandtown first. There's a little alley street there. At the end of it you look towards Sparrows Point and all these little row houses. And I just remember Rockwell saying, "Necco® wafers"—the colors. And they all started sketching. Then we would just sit there. We were like insurance agents. We looked like cops out spying on people. But I'm used to that. When I write, I always drive around. I showed them where we filmed all the scenes in the movie. Then we went to Pigtown, we went to Hampden, all my favorite neighborhoods.

ML: Where is Pigtown? I've never heard of these places.

Was that around when I was growing up?

JW: Of course it was! You were just a good girl from the right side of the tracks before Broadway corrupted you. Anyway, we went to Pigtown and we made this turn. It's a dead end, right where it looks like there's an abandoned factory, and there were the crackheads and us . . . ! I just started laughing, but I think all the hair went up on everyone else's necks. "Welcome to Baltimore," I said. It was kind of like *Night of the Living Dead,* but in a good way. The dealers were coming over towards our car, but they seemed nice enough. We just drove away.

I think, coming to Baltimore, you sort of have to see parts of the city to believe your eyes. People come to town and say to me "Now I see. You make documentaries. I always thought your movies were really exaggerated fantasies, but now I see, they are real."

In December 2001, two full-length readings of the musical were presented at New York's Westbeth Theatre Center. Lion and her partners raised the show's entire $10.5 million budget that day.

JW: You even said to me that, in all your theater past, you had never had this happen before. People were throwing money at you.

ML: What an exhilarating day that was. I couldn't believe it. We even made our final casting decisions between the two readings.

JW: That was the day when I said, "All of them. Go with every single one. You're crazy—you raised the whole budget in one day. You want to get rid of somebody?"

ML: You were very concerned. And you kept saying, "Stop! You're going to ruin it if you make changes."

JW: I said, "What are you looking for? You've got 'em. You found 'em. It's shocking that Bernie Telsey, the casting director, and you found the actors so easily and quickly."

ML: Hey, and we agreed.

Six months later, Hairspray *played an exclusive pre-Broadway engagement at Seattle's 5th Avenue Theatre.*

ML: Right out of the gate, Seattle showed us that audiences loved the show.

JW: But the book changed, too. And that's what's supposed to happen in previews. The writers worked out a lot of things and it's a hit because of it. I think the best change is when Link [Tracy's boyfriend] leaves her, and Tracy really is hurt and you really feel bad for her, and then she decides to go forward with the protest. That never happens in the movie, and it's a very good rewrite because it adds something else. Tracy loses something and gets it back, and you believe it. That's when I think the whole book totally clicked, from that scene.

ML: We all recognized that we needed to delay Tracy's dream to create some suspense, to have a better dramatic arc.

JW: In the movie, it doesn't happen. But it should have. When writers get to do a play inspired by a movie, it is already a second rewrite. Hindsight is a big luxury.

Waters's research for the 1988 film began with an article on The Buddy Deane Show *he had written for* Baltimore *magazine three years earlier. He also relied on personal experience; he had been on the show several times.*

JW: I went on with Mary Vivian Pearce, who starred in my early films, and who could have cared less about *The Buddy Deane Show*. I remember she flicked cigarette butts into one of the Committee member's beehives. We got thrown off for doing the Dirty Boogie at the Timonium State Fair when the show went on location—not thrown off, but they said we couldn't dance like that. Oh, and I was on another time but it wasn't on television, it was a record hop. I won the Twist contest, and the prize was the album *Do the Twist with Ray Charles*, which I still have.

In real life, *The Buddy Deane Show* had a very sad ending. It didn't get integrated, it just went off the air. Buddy was fair about it. It was mostly the white kids' parents who said, "You're not dancing with black kids on television." In real life, what happened is that the girl who ironed her hair in the movie snuck onto the show with other integrationists, but the station pulled the plug, and the show was over.

I remember being obsessed by the show for many years afterwards. My friends and I used to come back to my apartment from the bars twenty years later and do all the dances, half-drunk—the Madison, the Roach, the New Continental. The police even came once, I remember, because the neighbors complained about the noise. Then there was this *Buddy Deane* reunion. It was the first one they had. And I went by myself because I thought no one

Indefatigable songwriters Scott Wittman and Marc Shaiman are probably discussing some fine point of showbiz with producer Margo Lion.

* Edna sells design label to Sears, plans to devote more time to her chicken and waffles.
* Velma is forgotten and alone but still very rich, so don't feel sorry for her.

1973
* Kung fu fighting finally resolves Vietnam conflict.
* Inez drops "Little" from her name.

1974
* Nation's fashions are too embarrassing to describe.
* Link and Tracy help Liz and Dick reconcile.

1975
* Link and Tracy finally marry, heralding end of hippie era.

1976
* Corny is elected governor of California, initiates "more music, less talk" policy.
* Motormouth Maybelle is elected queen of Maryland (office created for her), legalizes the Dirty Boogie.
* Tracy and Link tour Middle East as "Ambassadors of Love," quit when paperwork proves excessive.

1977
* Freak curling-iron accident makes Penny a genius; she panics briefly after she realizes Carter is president.
* Fashion model Inez opens chic eatery on West 125th Street in Manhattan.

1978
* Penny and Seaweed go to law school together.
* Shirley Temple and Velma both turn fifty.

1979
* Studio 54—and disco in general—are getting very tired.
* Wilbur is briefly tired, feels better after nap.

11

cares about this but me. Anybody I'd bring who wasn't obsessed by it would have had a horrible time—it was impossible to explain. So I went, and I was like a fan at a Beatles concert. I thought, Oh, my God, I haven't seen these people in twenty years. There's Mary Lou! There's Gene and Linda Snyder! There's Vicki Defeo! I wrote that article about the reunion for *Baltimore* magazine really only as an excuse for my nosiness and voyeurism.

ML: It was a riveting article.

JW: Thank you. I really got into it. I was having a really hard time in my career in those years. I hadn't made a movie in eight years. I had made *Polyester*, which was a success, and then I tried to make the sequel to *Pink Flamingos*, which I shouldn't have, and I tried too long. Nobody would finance it. I know now that if you attempt to raise the money for a movie and it doesn't work in two years, give up. Come back to it later, which is what happened with *Cecil B. Demented*, and it finally got produced. I thought I had to do something really, really different and the idea of *Hairspray* just came to me. But, believe me, I had no idea of trying to make a commercial PG movie. I thought it would be rated NC-17 just because it was Divine and me. There was no conscious decision to write differently. It just was that, for once, normal people liked one of my obsessions. It was a fluke.

ML: I have to confess I never anticipated that the musical would be such a popular family show. But I should have. You told me right from the start that *Hairspray* was big with the twelve-year-old slumber party set.

JW: And children's birthday parties, too. Which shocked me the first time I heard it. But I thought, Why not? Little kids don't even know Divine was a man.

The filmmaker and producer agree that although Hairspray *is a comedy, it has serious themes, albeit with a John Waters twist.*

JW: For me it was always: the outsider wins, and integration prevails. The fat girl stood for gay, black, crippled—all outsiders that society rejects. You're not supposed to say crippled now—physically challenged. But what is fat now? It's called weight-challenged, or ample.

ML: And for me—now, John, don't faint—*Hairspray* is a celebration of the best of American values. It celebrates diversity and inclusion and the power of the individual to change the world. But—and here's the fun of it—the realization of those values is subversive.

JW: But it was a comedy about integration, which was awkward for a white man to do. And I was nervous about it because, before, I had made *Desperate Living* and lesbians stopped it from being shown. "How dare a man make a comedy about lesbians?" they complained. And now lesbian groups show it to raise money on college campuses, which I think is great.

America's tastes have changed. *Hairspray* proves it. I almost choke on these words but it's true—it's a big hit. It's about the teenage white girl who gets a black guy. The fat girl gets a straight guy, and her mother's a man who sings a love song to another man.

ML: Bravo! Look at the lineup of those characters at the curtain call. It brings a lump to your throat.

JW: The only people who aren't on stage are the so-called "normal" people.

ML: This is true.

JW: There's not one normal character in the cast. There isn't.

ML: Or probably off in the wings, either.

Before Hairspray, *Lion had produced a number of critically and popularly acclaimed shows, including* Angels in America *and* Jelly's Last Jam. *But they didn't tip the instant-megahit scale like* Hairspray.

JW: Are people pitching you now more than ever?

ML: Oh, you know, for fifteen minutes I'm the oracle. The truth is I want to have fun with this wondrous new child; there is still a lot to do to make sure that she grows up well. And, John, I told you when you're ready for your children's movie, I want to produce it.

JW: See, but I'm doing a movie about sex addicts next.

ML: But after that it's a children's movie, right?

JW: Keep 'em surprised. Keep 'em guessing. Especially after *Hairspray*, I'm really glad I'm doing a sex-addict movie. If I tried to make a really sweet movie now, it would be badly received, I think. The timing would not be good, because I also have to follow the great success that this play has had. And, you know, I'm going to have "overexposed" tattooed on my forehead. People yell to me on the street now, "Thank you!" I feel like a twisted Oprah.

ML: That really threw me. I had hoped the show would recoup its investment and have a life, particularly in high schools and amateur companies. I never thought, ever, that it would . . .

JW: . . . that it would be *Cats* for fat people.

ML: There are people who have been back to this show five and six times. It's like a drug. Endorphins flood the theater every night, and the audience goes out flying. Joy, that's the only word for it.

JW: I've also seen lots of fat mothers with their daughters watching it, which is touching in a way I hadn't imagined.

ML: Ohhh. And I love it that there are eight-year-olds, girls *and* boys, dancing in the aisle during the finale.

As the day drew to a close, Waters and Lion discussed the ways in which Hairspray's *success has affected them personally. Both mentioned family.*

JW: Thank God, my parents were there to see this, because they have been through many ups and downs in my career. You know—I must admit it gets on my nerves—when I'm in Baltimore all these people come up to me and say, "We love your movies." They don't love them *all*. They love *Hairspray*. So I tell them, "You liked *Multiple Maniacs*? I don't think so. You should go rent *Pink Flamingos*, you'd like that." And even my mother said, people that used to ask about my brother and sisters and not mention my name, as if I was dead, now say, "You must be so proud." And it irks her. She remembers, too. Right?

But to have my parents there opening night, on Broadway, which was astounding to me, much less them. And my mom was on the cover of the *Baltimore Sun* the next day with a quote that made me think she is starting to do sound bites quite well, which is frightening. She said, "People always say to me, 'What do you think of your son's movies?' And I always joked, 'I'm waiting for him to make the next *Sound of Music*.' Well, he did, and it's better."

And the other great thing that happened that night was before the play started. I was sitting there, you know, everyone's nervous. Harvey Fierstein's mom came over, introduced herself, and said to my mom, "Didn't we raise terrific sons?"—which is a loaded statement. But what a great thing to say.

ML: I never allowed myself to dream this dream; I just wanted to continue working in the theater without going belly-up. And in a remarkable twist of fate, I'm celebrating the city I thought was forever out of my life. The truth is, it's a miracle.

JW: It's like Dorothy at the end of *The Wizard of Oz*: you had to go home, Margo. You had to get your Baltimore roots touched up.

Act One
Prologue

(The CURTAIN rises on TRACY TURNBLAD in her bed. The time is around 7 A.M. on a Monday morning in early June 1962.)

"GOOD MORNING BALTIMORE"

The first image, the choreographic image, in a musical can transport an audience from its seats to a place of excitement and anticipation of what's to come.

In Hairspray, this moment came to me just as it appears on stage. I had been doing preproduction and I was eating, drinking, and sleeping the score. The music was in my blood.

One morning I woke up in my bed singing "Good Morning Baltimore" staring at my ceiling . . . that was it!

This was the image, the way to start the show. It was powerful, it matched the music, it was "off-center," very John Waters, and it was fun. It allowed me to put dancing shadows all around Tracy's head and invite the audience into Tracy's world of dreams.

—Jerry Mitchell

TRACY

OH, OH, OH,
WOKE UP TODAY
FEELING THE WAY I ALWAYS DO
OH, OH, OH,
HUNGRY FOR SOMETHING THAT I CAN'T EAT
THEN I HEAR THE BEAT

THAT RHYTHM OF TOWN
STARTS CALLING ME DOWN
IT'S LIKE A MESSAGE FROM HIGH ABOVE
OH, OH, OH,
PULLING ME OUT
TO THE SMILES AND THE STREETS THAT I LOVE

	BACKUP
GOOD MORNING BALTIMORE	GOOD MORNING BALTIMORE
EVERY DAY'S LIKE AN OPEN DOOR	
	AAH - AAH . . .
EVERY NIGHT IS A FANTASY	FANTASY
EVERY SOUND'S LIKE A SYMPHONY	
GOOD MORNING BALTIMORE	GOOD MORNING BALTIMORE
AND SOME DAY	
WHEN I TAKE TO THE FLOOR	OOH - OOH
THE WORLD'S GONNA WAKE UP AND SEE	AAH - SEE - EE
BALTIMORE AND ME	
OH, OH, OH,	HOOT
LOOK AT MY HAIR	HOO - OOT
WHAT "DO" CAN COMPARE	
WITH MINE TODAY?	. . . MINE TODAY
OH, OH, OH,	
HOOT	
I'VE GOT MY HAIRSPRAY AND RADIO	
I'M READY TO GO	. . . READY TO GO
THE RATS ON THE STREET	OOH - OOH
ALL DANCE 'ROUND MY FEET	OOH - OOH
THEY SEEM TO SAY	OOH
TRACY, IT'S UP TO YOU	. . . UP TO YOU

The show's string section isn't in the pit but in a separate room in the basement. Funny, friendly music director Lon Hoyt conducts them via closed-circuit television.

Early in the rehearsal, the rats were played by slickly-dressed humans—it was deemed too "Disney."

So, these marginal notes are kind of like the spoken commentary on DVDs, huh?

Yeah . . . Mark and Tom's comments are in purple boxes and Marc and Scott's comments are in pink boxes.

Marc and Scott wanted to write a John Waters version of "Oh, What a Beautiful Morning" from Oklahoma! This was the first song written for the score.

RHYMES WITH "BALTIMORE"

bore	* bar the door	* top floor	sycamore	roar
boar	* doggie door	* bottom floor	amour	* lion's roar
* wild boar	* trap door	* have the floor	sophomore	uproar
	outdoor	before		
chore	corridor	therefore	nor	sore
* household chore	Labrador	wherefore	ignore	* canker sore
corps	toreador	heretofore	manure	* eyesore
* Peace Corps	adore	metaphor	snore	* saddle sore
* Marine Corps	pompadour	petit four		* footsore
core	troubador	pinafore	or	* heartsore
* to the core	Ecuador		* either or	soar
* apple core	matador	gore	warrior	dinosaur
hardcore	drawer	* blood and gore	posterior	store
softcore	* dresser drawer		oar	* discount store
encore	* top drawer	abhor		* mind the
albacore		whore	poor	store
décor	coiffure		* rich or poor	* ten cent store
liqueur	for	galore	* dirt poor	* girl next door
	* falling for	lore	pour	score
door	* hoping for	folklore	* downpour	* man o' war
* open door	* praying for		pore	* act of war
* door to door	* waiting for	anymore	deplore	* world war
* swinging door	four	nevermore	implore	* anti-war
* back door	ten-four	forever more	explore	yore
* stage door	floor	furthermore	rapport	days of yore
* at death's	* dance floor	Barrymore		señor
door	* take the floor	paramour		you're

The Bum

These lyrics are why this song differs from most city anthems.

"FEAR OF JOHN WATERS"
A producer was upset about actually "seeing" the flasher onstage... We ended up cutting his actual flashing of Tracy to pacify him.

TRACY (cont'd)	BACKUP (cont'd)
SO, OH, OH,	
DON'T HOLD ME BACK	
'CAUSE TODAY	. . . TODAY
ALL MY DREAMS WILL COME TRUE	ALL MY DREAMS WILL COME TRUE
GOOD MORNING BALTIMORE	GOOD MORNING BALTIMORE
THERE'S THE FLASHER	
WHO LIVES NEXT DOOR	AAH - AAH
THERE'S THE BUM	
ON HIS BARROOM STOOL	. . . BARROOM STOOL
THEY WISH ME LUCK ON MY WAY TO SCHOOL	
GOOD MORNING BALTIMORE	GOOD MORNING BALTIMORE
AND SOME DAY	
WHEN I TAKE TO THE FLOOR	OOH - OOH
THE WORLD'S GONNA WAKE UP AND SEE	WAH
	SEE
BALTIMORE AND ME	
I KNOW EVERY STEP	HOOT
	HOO-OOT
I KNOW EVERY SONG	
	HOO - OOT
I KNOW THERE'S A PLACE	
WHERE I BELONG	WHERE I BELONG
I SEE ALL THE PARTY LIGHTS	HOOT
SHINING AHEAD	HOO -OOT
SO SOMEONE INVITE ME	
BEFORE I DROP DEAD	
	BEFORE SHE DROPS DEAD
SO, OH, OH,	OOH
GIVE ME A CHANCE	OOH - OOH
'CAUSE WHEN I START TO DANCE	
I'M A MOVIE STAR	MOVIE STAR
OH, OH, OH,	OOH - OOH
SOMETHING INSIDE OF ME	
MAKES ME MOVE	MAKES ME MOVE
WHEN I HEAR THAT GROOVE	WHEN I HEAR THAT GROOVE

Thank YOU, don't SUE! "Good Morning Baltimore"—"Oh, What a Beautiful Morning" meets "Be My Baby"

...presenting the fabulous RONETTES featuring VERONICA

17

TRACY (cont'd)	BACKUP (cont'd)
MY MA TELLS ME NO,	OOH - OOH
BUT MY FEET TELL ME GO	OOH - OOH
IT'S LIKE A DRUMMER	OOH
INSIDE MY HEART	. . . SIDE MY HEART
OH, OH, OH,	
DON'T MAKE ME WAIT	
ONE MORE MOMENT	ONE MORE MOMENT
FOR MY LIFE TO START	FOR MY LIFE TO START
	GOOD MORNING
	GOOD MORNING
	WAITING FOR MY LIFE TO START
I LOVE YOU BALTIMORE	I LOVE YOU BALTIMORE
EVERY DAY'S LIKE AN OPEN DOOR	
EVERY NIGHT IS A FANTASY	AAH - AAH . . . FANTASY
EVERY SOUND'S LIKE A SYMPHONY	
AND I PROMISE BALTIMORE	I PROMISE BALTIMORE
THAT SOME DAY	
WHEN I TAKE TO THE FLOOR	TAKE TO THE FLOOR
THE WORLD'S GONNA WAKE UP AND SEE	WAH . . . SEE
GONNA WAKE UP AND SEE	GONNA WAKE UP AND SEE
BALTIMORE AND ME,	
	YES, MORE OR LESS WE ALL AGREE
BALTIMORE AND ME	
	SOMEDAY THE WORLD IS GONNA SEE
BALTIMORE AND ME . . .	. . . AND ME . . .

Somehow we segue from morning to four o'clock in the afternoon.

It Started in Seattle

Jack O'Brien, Director

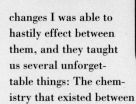

So many people, staggering out of *Hairspray*, their faces practically frozen in myriad expressions of joy, have asked, "How did you manage to get all that in?" In other words, a musical entertainment that basically pretends to be nothing more than that also seems to suggest overtones of social responsibility, a slight satiric edge, and the overwhelming aura of sheer nostalgic innocent belief, none of which necessarily goes hand in hand with the essential components of, well, a musical entertainment. How is that possible?

I have a simple answer: Seattle!

But I must begin with a disclaimer: I was one of the last people hired for *Hairspray*, at least so far as the creative team is concerned. This musical delirium, which began with a cornucopia of songs that tumbled from the musical brains of Marc Shaiman and Scott Wittman, with an original book originally fashioned breathlessly afterwards by Mark O'Donnell, had various workshops and readings before either Jerry Mitchell, the choreographer and my alter ego, or I joined the team. There were songs, lyrics, versions of the book; there were demos recorded by various artists, none of whom showed up in the final production; there were relationships with young singers eager to be part of this mix that were formed and socially solidified long

before I ever sat down with either the creators or those they had already chosen to surround themselves with. My initial impression was of a torrent of activity, talents, opinions, prejudices, and efforts, all converging on one rather remarkable afternoon when we sat before perhaps a couple hundred of our nearest and dearest and simply read what we thought might be the best version of our evolving show. Before that, various component parts of the team had gathered in various living rooms for various nefarious purposes, but nothing specific comes to mind; nothing consequential seemed to stand out before those two contiguous readings erupted in more happy laughter and sustained ovations of delight I can ever remember hearing.

The world of *Hairspray* as we know it now really began for me on that chilly gray afternoon as the two invited audiences climbed the staircase to the obligatory rows of empty chairs at Westbeth. The readings were, in fact, nearly identical, except for the dozen or so notes and/or line changes I was able to hastily effect between them, and they taught us several unforgettable things: The chemistry that existed between Harvey Fierstein as Edna and Dick Latessa as Wilbur was something directly from the gods. The show was funnier than we ever had a right to believe. The music was every bit as sensational as we had thought it was. And Marissa Winokur clearly had the chops, the charm, and the stamina to do two performances of that tyro, Tracy, in one day. Who knew?

We were off and running.

But back to Seattle! All shows come together in ostensibly the same manner—you teach the music, you gingerly begin blocking the acting scenes, and you routine the musical numbers with the dogged tenacity of Marine drill instructors. It's hard, grim, often debilitating work, and

whether it's Shakespeare or Sondheim it has a profile that isn't remarkably dissimilar. But, eventually, you stagger through an act here, an act there, and some anomalous, elephantine shape begins to appear. Where there was once a string of two-dimensional scenes linking evidently exhausting dance routines, suddenly an entire strand of something remarkably lifelike and comprehensible appears. You may have a show after all!

So we did, at this point, the only sane thing either Jerry Mitchell or I know how to do: We went away. Far away. To the Fifth Avenue Theatre in lovely, summery Seattle, during which time it shed its reputation of being nothing but rain-rain-rain and became something so blithe and beautiful it's hard to believe rain ever existed. We sat down and burrowed our way through the endless, boring, deeply complicated series of technical rehearsals until we finally faced our first preview audience, before which we all resolutely gathered, knuckles collectively whitened, shoulders hunched in rigid tension, and then . . . And then . . .

That very first audience flipped. And at the sustained build that ends with "You Can't Stop the Beat," they stood and cheered and cheered and cheered. The next night the same thing happened. And on the third performance, there happened to be something of a benefit audience that went so wild with delight that the company, having adjourned after the curtain call to their respective

dressing rooms and having changed into their street clothes, were staggered to realize the audience was still below in the theater, stomping and cheering, and so Harvey Fierstein, half-dressed and only half himself, was persuaded to go back down to confront them. Wow!

But it was a benefit, wasn't it? And after all, it was Seattle!

And so it went, performance after performance, week after week. We got better and better; we continued to work, to refine, to rewrite, to shape, to condense, to zero in on laughs and moments and, yes, zero in on and protect a sense of reality, too, and through it all, the audiences went bonkers. Just bonkers. But down in some deep, private part of us, we didn't really believe it. After all, it was Seattle! And when we would get to New York, naturally . . .

Now, as I have spent most of the last two decades doing some of my best work as artistic director at the Globe Theatres in San Diego, I was nevertheless somewhat suspicious of dismissing these uproarious, delighted audiences as being "just Seattle." I knew better. I had taken several shows from the west coast to the east, and my experience had taught me that it was often tougher to get enthusiasm out there than on Broadway, curious as that may seem. Displaced easterners, now living all over the globe, are often suspicious that what you are offering them might not be what

they were used to when they lived in or near Manhattan, and they give their enthusiasm most begrudgingly. So if you get laughs in San Diego, or Seattle, or Timbuktu, for that matter, they are dearly earned and probably worthy of the event.

So what beautiful Seattle offered us was a kind of bell jar of innocence. The company was encouraged to play not for laughs, and not for the audience's approval, but rather for each other—since no one could afford to take the ovations and the roars of laughter altogether seriously.

We did our work, we believed as best we could in what we were creating, and we left the rest of the details to fate. A bell jar it was, of both innocence and integrity, and none of us was aware of having lowered it over our company, over the Fifth Avenue Theatre, over Seattle. We were displaced actors, dancers, musicians, writers, and, after all, yes, it was Seattle!

And so it is. And it is finally Seattle I personally have to thank, for the generosity of spirit, the patience, the hospitality, and for teaching us, finally, that playing for ourselves—for each other, in fact, may just be the best direction one can ever achieve.

Act One
Scene 1

(TV station WZZT and the TURNBLAD home simultaneously. Monday afternoon.)

As a teenager, John Waters danced on The Buddy Deane Show, Baltimore's real-life model for The Corny Collins Show.

CORNY	BACKUP
Hey there, teenage Baltimore!	OH-OO-OO-OO-OO-OO-OO-OO
Don't change that channel!	OH-OO-OO-OO-OO-OO-OO-OO
'Cause it's time for *The Corny*	OH-OO-OO-OO-OO-OO-OO-OO
Collins Show! Brought to you by	HOOT HOOT HOOT HOO-OOT
Ultra Clutch Hairspray! For hair	
that holds up even in a NASA	
wind tunnel!	
EV'RY AFTERNOON	
WHEN THE CLOCK STRIKES FOUR	
	BOP-BEE-BA, BA-BA-BA-BA, BEE-BA
A CRAZY BUNCH OF KIDS	
CRASH THROUGH THAT DOOR, YEAH	
	BOP-BEE-BA, BA-BA-BA-BA, BEE-BA
THEY THROW OFF THEIR COATS	OW-OOT
AND LEAVE THE SQUARES BEHIND	HOOT, OW-OOT
AND THEN THEY SHAKE IT,	
SHAKE IT, SHAKE IT	
LIKE THEY'RE LOSING THEIR MIND	OW-OOT, OW-OOT
YOU'LL NEVER SEE THEM FROWN	
'CAUSE THEY'RE	
THE NICEST KIDS IN TOWN	. . . NICEST KIDS IN TOWN
EVERY AFTERNOON	
YOU TURN YOUR TV ON	
	NA, NA, NA, NA, NA,
	NA-NA-NA-NA
AND WE KNOW YOU	
TURN THE SOUND UP	
WHEN YOUR PARENTS ARE GONE	
	NA, NA, NA, NA, NA, NA-NA-NA-NA
AND THEN YOU	
TWIST AND SHOUT	OOH
FOR YOUR FAVORITE STAR	OOH
AND ONCE YOU'VE	
PRACTICED EVERY STEP	OOH
THAT'S IN YOUR REPERTOIRE	OOH
YOU BETTER COME ON DOWN	OOH
AND MEET THE	
NICEST KIDS IN TOWN	. . . NICEST KIDS IN TOWN

TRACY

Hurry, Penny, hurry–the show's already started! We're gonna miss it!

PENNY

I'm hurrying, Tracy, but my mother says I'm not allowed to perspire!

TRACY

C'mon!

PRUDY

Edna, is my laundry ready?

EDNA

(EDNA is slaving away at her ironing board next to a huge stack of laundry. PRUDY is picking up her laundry.)
Who wants to know? Sure it is, hun. Come on up. That'll be three dollars.

PRUDY

(digging in her purse)
That's pretty pricey for a few pairs of pettipants.

EDNA

I'm sorry, Prudy Pingleton, but there were some extra charges. Some of your personal stains required pounding on a rock. *(TRACY and PENNY enter.)*

TRACY

I'm home!

EDNA

Four o'clock. Guess I don't need to ask who got detention again. Tracy Turnblad, mind your manners and say hello to our guest.

TRACY

Hello, Mrs. Pingleton.

EDNA

And you, Penny?

PENNY

Hello, Mrs. Pingleton . . . I mean . . . Mother.

This replaced "Sorry! Its hard to run and chew gum at the same time!"

In previews, Harvey got so much applause for his entrance that Jackie Hoffman, as PRUDY, sat down until it finally stopped.

COMEDY THEORY: Alliteration is said to be funny.

We decided "personal stains" manages to be discreet and tasteless at the same time.

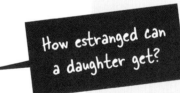

How estranged can a daughter get?

EDNA
(to PRUDY)
Teenagers. They just love watching that Corny Collins.

PRUDY

Delinquents. It ain't right dancing to that colored music.

EDNA

Don't be silly, ain't colored. The TV's black and white.
(PRUDY exits with her bundle, shaking her head in disapproval.)

 CUT

"This Week magazine says listening to rock and roll can lead to . . . flippancy!!"

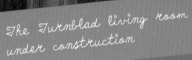

The Turnblad living room under construction

some inspiration for the Turnblad teevee

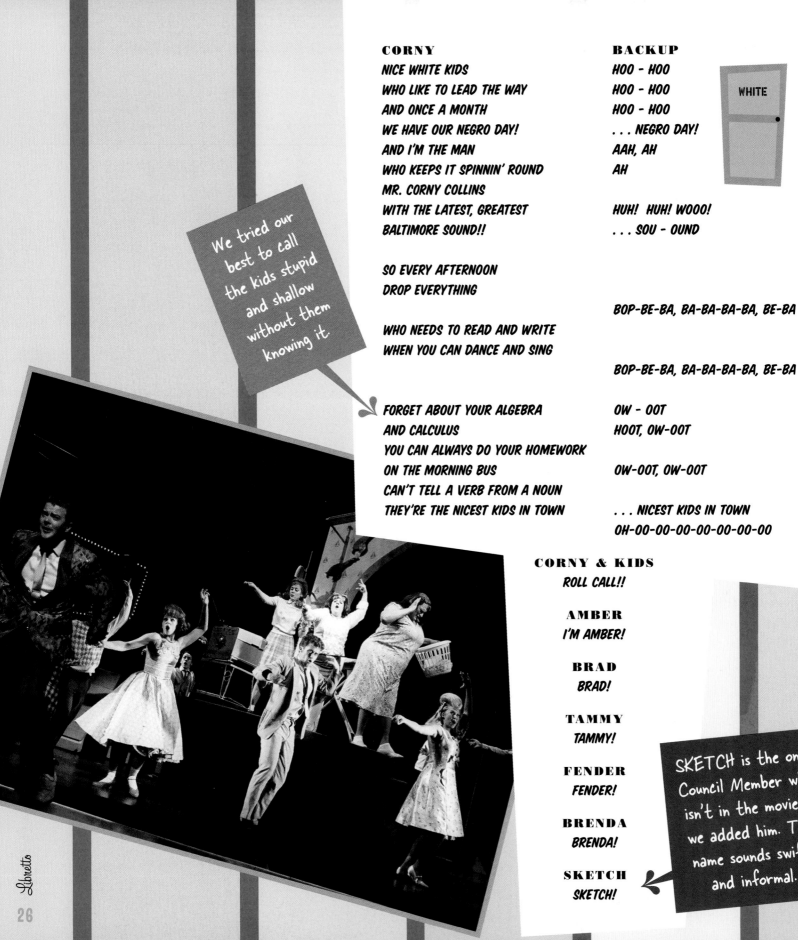

CORNY

NICE WHITE KIDS
WHO LIKE TO LEAD THE WAY
AND ONCE A MONTH
WE HAVE OUR NEGRO DAY!
AND I'M THE MAN
WHO KEEPS IT SPINNIN' ROUND
MR. CORNY COLLINS
WITH THE LATEST, GREATEST
BALTIMORE SOUND!!

SO EVERY AFTERNOON
DROP EVERYTHING

WHO NEEDS TO READ AND WRITE
WHEN YOU CAN DANCE AND SING

FORGET ABOUT YOUR ALGEBRA
AND CALCULUS
YOU CAN ALWAYS DO YOUR HOMEWORK
ON THE MORNING BUS
CAN'T TELL A VERB FROM A NOUN
THEY'RE THE NICEST KIDS IN TOWN

BACKUP

HOO - HOO
HOO - HOO
HOO - HOO
. . . NEGRO DAY!
AAH, AH
AH

HUH! HUH! WOOO!
. . . SOU - OUND

BOP-BE-BA, BA-BA-BA-BA, BE-BA

BOP-BE-BA, BA-BA-BA-BA, BE-BA

OW - OOT
HOOT, OW-OOT

OW-OOT, OW-OOT

. . . NICEST KIDS IN TOWN
OH-OO-OO-OO-OO-OO-OO-OO

CORNY & KIDS
ROLL CALL!!

AMBER
I'M AMBER!

BRAD
BRAD!

TAMMY
TAMMY!

FENDER
FENDER!

BRENDA
BRENDA!

SKETCH
SKETCH!

WHITE   COLORED

We tried our best to call the kids stupid and shallow without them knowing it.

SKETCH is the only Council Member who isn't in the movie— we added him. The name sounds swift and informal.

SHELLEY
SHELLEY!

IQ
IQ!

LOU ANN
LOU ANN!

LINK
AND I'M . . . LINK!

Act One, Scene 1

27

✂ CUT

TRACY: I love this show more than life itself!

PENNY: Me too! Sometimes I think I don't even deserve to watch it!

This is an amusing line from the movie that is made much funnier by Divine's voice and delivery. We used it as an example one day in a casting session to underline the importance of getting an actor for EDNA with a distinctive voice. Enter, Harvey Fierstein.

TRACY

Oh, Link, kiss me again and again.

EDNA

Turn that racket down. I'm trying to iron in here.

CORNY	BACKUP
SO, IF EVERY NIGHT YOU'RE SHAKING	AAH
AS YOU LIE IN BED	AAH
	MONY-MONY, OOH, MONY-MONY
AND THE BASS AND DRUMS	AAH, AAH, AAH, AAH
ARE POUNDING IN YOUR HEAD	
	MONY-MONY, OOH, MONY-MONY
WHO CARES ABOUT SLEEP	HOW - OOT!
WHEN YOU CAN SNOOZE IN SCHOOL	
	HOOT, OW - OOT
THEY'LL NEVER GET TO COLLEGE	
BUT THEY SURE LOOK COOL	
	OW - OOT, OW - OOP!
DON'T NEED A CAP AND A GOWN	
'CAUSE THEY'RE THE	
NICEST KIDS IN TOWN	. . . NICEST KIDS IN TOWN
THEY'RE THE	OH-OO-OO-OO-OO-OO-OO-OO
NICEST, NICEST	OH-OO-OO-OO-OO-OO-OO-OO
THEY'RE THE	OH-OO-OO-OO-OO-OO-OO-OO
NICEST, NICEST	OH-OO-OO-OO-OO-OO-OO-OO
THEY'RE THE	
SUGAR AND SPICE-EST, NICEST	. . . KIDS IN
KIDS IN TOWN	KIDS IN TOWN - HOOT!

For the record, MONY rhymes with PONY, not with HONEY.

CORNY

And that was our new dance of the week—the Stricken Chicken. We'll be right back.
(*Lights shift in the TV studio.*)

This dance we invented—but the Mashed Potato was real!

VELMA

And we're off! All right, people, how many times do I have to tell you—we do NOT touch ourselves—any-where—while on camera. Tammy, lose the padding. You too, Fender.
(*The KIDS sheepishly turn away to remove their padding.*)
And, Link, stop hogging the camera; you're not Elvis yet. Amber . . . hog the camera.

AMBER

Yes, Mother.

VELMA

And YOU, Mr. Collins! None of that Detroit sound today. You have some-thing against Connie Francis?

This replaced "They'll dance to Guy Lombardo if I say so!"

VELMA combines three characters from the movie: Debbie Harry's pushy stage mom; Mink Stole, harried stage manager; and Divine's cameo as the bigoted station owner. Efficient, huh?

CORNY

The kids are just over the moon for rhythm and blues, Velma. They can't get enough.

VELMA

They're kids, Corny. That's why we have to steer them in the white direc-tion . . . I mean . . . you know what I mean.

LINK

Amber, I've got something for you.
(*offers his ring*)
I figured, since we've been going together sort of . . . steadily . . . maybe we should make it official.

Act One Scene 1

29

AMBER

Oh, Link. Your Council Member ring. How sweet. And it matches my hair color exactly.
(They kiss.)

VELMA

Ah, ah, ah! None of that! Save your personal lives for the camera! And we're back in five . . . four . . . three . . .
(The lights change to indicate that we're back on the air.)

CORNY

Now don't forget, guys and Gidgets—our very first prime-time spectacular is coming up on June 6th. We'll be live at Baltimore's brand-new Eventorium broadcasting nationwide!

CORNY

Talent scouts will be on hand from all of the major record labels, and sponsoring the event will be none other than our own ULTRA CLUTCH HAIRSPRAY. So, let's give a great big fawning Baltimore salute to the president of Ultra Clutch, Harriman F. Spritzer.
(SPRITZER nervously steps out and waves to the room.)

CUT
"And keep it caucasian!"

CUT
"It will make all those June weddings and traditions look pointless by comparison."

Baltimore exists, but we invented the Eventorium and Ultra Clutch.

So natural... even HE can't tell!

COMEDY THEORY: Characters' names reveal their natures and/or their jobs.

SPRITZER

Ultra Clutch is happy to bring you fine youngsters to national attention.

ALL

Our big break!

CORNY

Also, live on the special, we'll be crowning your choice for Miss Teenage Hairspray 1962!

AMBER

My big break!

EDNA

(looking at the television)
Well, isn't she a lovely slim girl.

TRACY

(to PENNY)
I guess Amber's pretty but she can't dance.

PENNY

Plastic little spastic.

TRACY

Oh, no! I'm gonna kill myself. Look! She's wearing Link's Council ring!

AMBER

(reading from a cue card)
Hey, gang, don't forget to watch Mom and me next Thursday on Mother-Daughter Day. And I want to be your Miss Teenage Hairspray. Remember, a vote for me from you is a vote for me.

"Age beside Beauty!"

CORNY

What an unexpected ad lib, Amber. And speaking of expecting the unexpected, our own fun-loving, free-wheeling Brenda will be taking a little leave of absence from the show. How long will you be gone, Brenda?

Tom wanted to make sure AMBER's speech verged on nonsensical.

BRENDA

Nine months.

This is BRENDA's only line, besides Roll Call and some gagging noises in Scene VI.

CUT

This song was inspired by cautionary films Scott saw in high school warning against drinking and driving, the most memorable of which was <u>The Last Prom</u>.

The cut public service announcement, sung by **LINK** and **AMBER.**

CORNY: Now, let's hear from that toothsome twosome, this area code's romantic answer to Sandra Dee and Bobby Darin, Amber and Link! (GIRLS scream, then MUSIC)

CORNY: They have a meaningful musical message for you all! Lay it on us, you pair of sweetniks!

"BLOOD ON THE PAVEMENT"

LINK
BLOOD ON THE PAVEMENT, WHAT A MESS!

AMBER
IS THAT YOUR EYEBALL ON MY DRESS?

AMBER & LINK
DON'T DRINK AND DRIVE
PLEASE KEEP YOUR HEAD

AMBER
OR COME GRADUATION DAY

AMBER & LINK
YOU'LL BE DEAD

LINK
PLEASE BUCKLE UP THOUGH I KNOW IT'S A DRAG
I'D HATE TO SEE THAT BODY IN A BODY BAG

VELMA
KIDS, LISTEN UP 'CAUSE I'M HER MOM

AMBER, LINK & VELMA
YES, BLOOD ON THE PAVEMENT WILL RUIN YOUR PROM!

CORNY

So, it seems we'll have an opening for a girl who is just as fun-loving, but maybe not quite as freewheeling. Wanna be one of the nicest kids in town? Cut school tomorrow and come on down to station WZZT to audition!

TRACY

Ohmigod! It's a dream of a lifetime. I have to go audition.

PENNY

Ohmigod! It's a dream of a lifetime. I have to go watch you audition.

EDNA

(snapping off the TV)
That'll be enough of that for one day. No one is auditioning for anything. There'll be no cutting school in this house.

PENNY

But Mrs. Turnblad . . .

EDNA

Penny, go tell your mother she wants you.

This was a standard schoolyard ploy in Mark's blue–collar Cleveland youth.

PENNY

She does? I better hurry. Bye, Mrs. Turnblad. Bye, Tracy. *(PENNY runs into WILBUR as he enters.)*

This replaced "That new shipment of rubber chickens is practically flying off the shelves!"

WILBUR

Whoa! Rush hour traffic! Hiya, ladies. Since I got that new shipment of exploding bubble gum, business downstairs is booming! How are my two funny honeys?

EDNA

Oh, stop, Wilbur. You're the funny one.

TRACY

Daddy, tomorrow I'm auditioning to dance on a TV show.

EDNA

You're going to have to go further than that to get around me, young lady. No one's auditioning for anything. And what did I tell you about that hair? All ratted up like a teenaged Jezebel.

LOST TO HISTORY
WILBUR: "Well, well! My own little June Taylor dancer!"
Nobody knew who the June Taylor Dancers were. (They performed on Jackie Gleason's 1960s TV show.)

TRACY

Mother, you are so fifties. Even our first lady, Jackie B. Kennedy, rats her hair.

EDNA

Yeah? Well, you ain't no first lady, are ya? She's a hair-hopper—that's what got her put in detention again.
(taking WILBUR aside)
Wilbur, talk to her. Girls like Tracy. . . People like us . . . You know what I'm saying. They don't put people like us on TV—except to be laughed at.

WILBUR

Tracy, this TV thing . . . You really want it?

TRACY

It's my dream, Daddy.

WILBUR

Then you go for it! This is America, babe. You gotta think big to be big.

A hair hopper is anyone who pays too much attention to their hair. Farrah Fawcett is an example of a 1970s-era hair hopper.

EDNA

Being big is not the problem, Wilbur.

WILBUR

When I was your age my parents begged me to run away with the circus, but I said, "No. That's what you want. I have dreams of my own." I dreamt of opening a chain of joke shops worldwide. So, okay, I've still only got one, but some day, if I can figure out how to keep the air from leaking out of my sofa-sized whoopee cushion, I'm going to make a noise heard 'round the world!
(EDNA screams with delight.)
You follow your dream, baby. I'm grabbin' an Orange Crush and heading back down to the Har-De-Har Hut. I've got my dream . . . and I wuv it!

EDNA

(laughing again)
You're not helping, Wilbur!
(WILBUR exits and TRACY follows.)

TRACY

Thanks, Daddy.

EDNA

Tracy, come back up here. I've got hampers of laundry and my diet pill is wearing off!

TRACY

But, Mama, I want to be famous.

EDNA

You want to be famous? Learn how to get blood out of car upholstery. Now that's a skill you could take right to the bank. You think I wanted to spend my life washing and ironing other people's clothing? No, I wanted to design them. I thought I would be the biggest thing in brassieres. Well, you deal with what life gives you. Now start folding.

TRACY

Ugh.
(Focus shifts to PENNY and PRUDY.)

PENNY

But, Mom, all I was doing was watching *Corny Collins* over at Tracy's.

One of the first Broadway musicals Scott saw was *The Education of H*Y*M*A*N K*A*P*L*A** in 1968, featuring Dick Latessa (WILBUR) at the Alvin Theater, now the Neil Simon Theatre and the home of Hairspray.

CUT

"I've got to go unload a shipment of dribble glasses, and that can be a tricky operation!"

This joke of Harvey's gets a big but delayed laugh.

✂ CUT
"Reader's Digest says that listening to music can actually make things happen in your brain!"

✂ CUT
"Your Pony was more like a Donkey!"

PRUDY

Didn't I forbid you from listening to race music? Oh, if the police ever locate your father he'll punish you good.
(Focus shifts to AMBER and VELMA.)

VELMA

Your dancing was atrocious today, Amber. I'm willing to lie, cheat, and steal to win you that Miss Hairspray crown, but you've got to work with me. Now let me at that zit!

EDNA

Stop! That's no way to treat clean clothes. One day you'll own "Edna's Occidental Laundry."
Will you be ready?

TRACY

I hope not.
(TRACY holds up an enormous pair of men's underpants.)

PRUDY

Don't contradict me!

VELMA

Don't disobey me!

EDNA

Don't even think about going to that audition.

GIRLS

Please!

MOMS

No!

GIRLS

Mother!!!!

MEET THE SUPREMES

The three girls have unwittingly just become a '60s-style girl group!

HAIRSPRAY E-MAILS HOME

by Harvey Fierstein

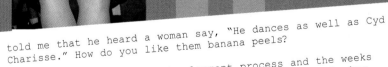

From: Harvey
To: Family & friends
Date: Friday, May 31, 2002 1:00 AM
Subject: First preview performance (Seattle, WA)

Okay folks, here's the only word I can use to describe what happened tonight . . . TRIUMPH!!!!! The audience laughed and screamed, hooted and hollered and carried on from curtain to curtain. They finished off by exploding into an amazing standing ovation the moment the lights went out. It was THRILLING!

All of this for a musical they had never heard of. I'd venture to say that most folks in the audience tonight had never even heard of HAIRSPRAY THE MOVIE not to mention HAIRSPRAY THE MUSICAL. They didn't know the songs but they practically sang along. The dances were all new, but that didn't stop the audience from trying to do them with us. What a night.

Now what does this mean in the long run? Who knows? But on this night, in Seattle, for 2,000 strangers, a new Musical Comedy Classic was born.

Tomorrow, I know, the producers will each have their notes followed by fixing and fighting and rewriting and revamping and CUTTING, I'm sure, but there is no denying that what we have achieved is what I think you'd have to call a good old-fashioned "Crowd Pleaser."

As for me, dear family and friends, I'm not exactly sure how to describe what I feel. When I rode out onto the stage tonight and the lights hit me, I heard a scream of delight that was heartwarming to say the least. From that moment, no matter what I did or said, whether I tripped over my dress or mistimed a laugh, the crowd was with me. I was carried for two and a half hours on the great good will of those people out there in the dark. There is simply no feeling like that to be had anywhere else than center stage. During the curtain call I looked over to Marissa and the poor dear was smiling so broadly that I thought her head might split in two. I took her hand and told her, "Welcome home, baby. From this moment you are now and forever more a Broadway star." We then, of course, held hands and cried.

But back to the performance . . . I wish you could have seen it all. You should have heard them shout when we did the quick-change from ugly ducking to swan. The roar was deafening. When Dick and I danced we could hardly hear the orchestra. That's how loudly the audience clapped along. Lon Hoyt

told me that he heard a woman say, "He dances as well as Cyd Charisse." How do you like them banana peels?

All through the two-year development process and the weeks of rehearsal I thought a lot about myself as a little boy who lip synched in his bedroom to his parents' cast albums. I was this strange little boy who dreamed of one day being Ethel Merman. Tonight, against all odds and reason, I was Ethel Merman. Tonight, as naïve as it sounds I am going to shout this to you: DREAM! You go the hell ahead and dream anything as big as you can imagine. Follow it up with good honest work, and I tell you all, it CAN COME TRUE.

Truth is, I am exhausted. The cast and crew are in the hotel bar downstairs celebrating, but I think I will keep to myself and reflect on how different this life of mine would now be had I not realized one moment of sanity six years ago and reached out to ask for the help I so desperately needed. I think I will stay upstairs in my room and take care of my many blessings: family, friends, animals, voice AND count my capacity for joy.

Love to you all. - Harvey

From: Harvey
To: Family & friends
Date: Saturday, June 1, 2002 12:30 AM
Subject: Second preview performance (Seattle, WA)

Okay gang, here's the skinny:

Tonight was the second performance which, as youse in the thee-ate-uh know, is traditionally a huge letdown. And after last night how could it not be so?

Well, children, there was no one let down in Seattle tonight!

If the audience went nuts last night, this audience went INSANE! There was simply no stopping some of the ovations and laughter. The show ran a full ten minutes longer than it had last night. We could do nothing wrong in the eyes of these folks.

The word-of-mouth is already beginning to spread around town and we can begin to feel the effect. There was a small crowd of autograph seekers waiting outside the stage door tonight that screamed with delight as each cast member appeared. My dressing room has a window overlooking that alley and I watched the whole scene undetected. Such fun!

The cast seems to revel in the positivity of it all. Some of them have never been in a hit show before. Maybe I shouldn't use the word HIT since we have no idea if the critics will understand what we are doing on that stage. I mean, how many critics do you know who claim to be fans of John Waters' work? Still, if this reaction continues and the word gets back to New York, we could actually build an advance and make ourselves critic-proof before they even see the show. Wouldn't that be lovely? But I find it almost impossible to imagine a single person not getting what we are doing here. Still the reality may be that these first two audiences are made up of HAIRSPRAY MOVIE fans and that's why they're reacting the way they do. Can't tell for sure. But tomorrow will show since we have our first double performances and I can't believe John Waters' fans go to matinees. We will see. Oh, and tomorrow night we have the SEATTLE MEN'S' CHORUS coming so I know that will be fun. But the matinee . . .?

Goodnight from Seattle where the hairspray is out of the can!

-Edna

From: Harvey
To: Family & friends
Date: Sunday, June 2, 2002 2:00 AM
Subject: Third and fourth preview performances (Seattle, WA)

As I sit down to write this latest letter I sincerely hope, from the bottom of my heart, that these notes are not coming off as bragging. What is happening to us in Seattle is truly amazing and I want to share it with you. All I can do is promise that I am NOT exaggerating. These are the facts as I am experiencing them and reporting them, unedited, to you back home.

I assumed our first matinee would be quiet and would allow us to clean up and focus again. Wrong! Although mellower than the first two night performances, the audience hooted and hollered and clapped as enthusiastically as any performer could wish. My fear of matinees was squelched. Once again we had proof that at very least we have a Crowd Pleaser on our hands. And then came tonight . . .

Okay, fourteen hundred seats were sold as a benefit for the SEATTLE MEN'S' CHORUS and eleven hundred seats went to regular folks. Since the chorus and I have a long history of performing together I expected a rousing welcome. What I got was something more. My first entrance stopped the show for almost a minute as they gave me an ovation the likes of which I haven't heard since the night I won my first TONY Award. It was thrilling for me. Of course the poor Council Kids had to keep vamping their dance the whole time. They looked ready to plotz by the time we could finally continue. But, continue we did. The audience ate every word as it came out of our mouths. We could do nothing wrong. Song after song brought the house down. Line after line elicited circus-style roars. By the time we reached the bows the cheering was feverish. Deafening. What a wonderful night. A triumphant first double show for us all.

So, the lights came down and we all left the stage, climbing the staircase back to our dressing rooms, laughing and joking and congratulating each other on the terrific show. Before getting undressed, I stopped by Dick's dressing room to rib

him about getting a lyric wrong in our song, then I stopped into the office to see who was around, and finally headed back to my dressing room, shoes in hand. Keith started unzipping that monstrous red gown when an announcement came over the P.A. system: "Harvey, could you please return to stage level. The audience will not leave." I thought that there was a raucous crowd gathering at the stage door and I figured they needed me to stick my head out, say hello, and disperse the gang. So, I went to my window and looked out but the alley was empty. Not a soul waiting. What was going on?

Again the announcement. "Harvey please return to the stage. Immediately. Please."

Something must be wrong onstage, I thought. I walked down the hall, climbed down the stairs to stage level and crossed the backstage area in my bare feet. One of the stage managers, Marisha, waved me onto the stage. Unsure what for, I stepped out onto the deserted stage and what I witnessed knocked the wind right out of my body. There was not a single person in the aisles. Every seat was still occupied. The entire audience, as far as I could tell, had remained standing at their chairs applauding and calling my name demanding my return to the stage.

I stepped out into the light and a cheer rose like one more appropriate to a football game. I was shocked. I couldn't hold myself together and tears streamed down my cheeks. Pulling myself together I walked to the apron of the stage, took the longest, deepest bow I could manage in that red menace of a dress and my foot-high wig and said, "Thank you and good night" in American sign language. I waved goodbye, turned and fairly floated back off the stage.

Well, folks, that ain't something that happens every day. In fact, that ain't something that happens in most lifetimes. I know I owe the experience to that wonderful chorus being there, but still, it was a thrill beyond this performer's wildest imaginations. Linda Hart, in fact, said she hadn't seen anything like it since her days with Bette Midler. Ha!

So, friends, that is the state of things here in Seattle three days into this adventure. It's all beyond BEYOND and I am grateful for every second. I only wish that we were enjoying this together. I don't know what's ahead. The critics may slay us. New York audiences may find our brand of happiness too unsophisticated. The world could be a different place by the time we come home to Broadway. But for this moment, I cannot wish for more satisfaction. Look out your window. You probably see me smiling all the way in Brooklyn.

Until the next report.

-Ethel

DEAR DIARY
by Marissa Jaret Winokur

Dear Diary

◎ NOVEMBER 14, 1999, LOS ANGELES

…got a phone call today from Dan Jinks, my producer from American Beauty. He told me he heard through the "gay grapevine" that they were talking about making Hairspray the movie into a Broadway musical. MUST GET DETAILS! HOW cool would that be?

✂ APRIL 20, 2000, LOS ANGELES

So I was supposed to fly to North Carolina yesterday, but found out Marc Shaiman would meet me today regarding HAIRSPRAY!!! His house was soooo nice. It was so much fun! There were posters of movies he has scored and a lot of really cool Bette Midler stuff! OH MY GOD MARC SHAIMAN!!!!! I sang a few songs but talked more! I think he thought I was crazy but who cares? I SO WANT TO DO THIS!!!! ♡

MAY 7, 2000, NEW YORK

Today was the first day of the reading. Heard the opening number and just started crying … It's called GOOD MORNING BALTIMORE and I swear it is the most perfect number I have ever heard! I can't believe I get to sing this song !!! Perfect! I just LOVE everything about it! The other songs are fun, too, but after BALTIMORE … nothing compares!

♡ DECEMBER 7, 2001, NEW YORK

…Well, today went great. Margo was really nice. Jack was very cool. His energy was great and he seemed really excited. Although Margo showed him a picture of a girl who auditioned for them in Baltimore … for my role …yesterday … THAT I AM PLAYING TODAY! Ugh. Tomorrow we sing with Shaiman. I can't wait for him to hear what Eric and I have come up with for "Tracy's voice" … it only took us a year and a half! Wait, I can't believe they were auditioning people for my role yesterday! …

♡♡♡♡DECEMBER 14, 2001, NEW YORK ♡♡♡♡

I did it! I made it through both readings. I've never been so relieved. Margo said I should feel really good about it and to go home, relax, sleep some! They had a huge party for the entire cast. They sat me down, in their bedroom, at one point, and told me how proud of me they were. That meant more than they'll ever know. Even if the show never goes or goes without me, that's what I have been waiting to hear for 2 years. MY GOD … TOOK 'em long enough! …

☆ DECEMBER 23, 2001, NEW YORK

…This is all so crazy! Next year, at this time, I may be starring in a big Broadway show … ☆☆☆

DECEMBER 27, 2001, NEW YORK

…Well, I made it. I am on my way back to LA. I am so relieved and scared to death. What did I get myself into? I can't believe we closed the deal. How cool is that?! The part is finally mine. It is truly TRULY mine! How am I ever going to learn the dances? …

♡ JANUARY 13, 2002, NEW YORK ♡

…Oh my god, you'll never believe what was in my hotel when I arrived: A big basket of food! Chocolates, cookies, candy — all kinds of treats. Not flowers. Not fruit. Not wine OR champagne BUT a fucking basket of candy crap from The Producers with a nice note!!! How funny is that?! They're trying to get me fatter! I bet they'd send me Twinkies everyday if they'd think I'd eat 'em …

◎◎JANUARY 15, 2002, NEW YORK

Oh my God! The photo shoot was amazing! I can't believe that I shot the poster today. They told me that the poster, billboards and everything was going to be my face. Times Square included. MY FACE! We had so much fun. Jerry was teaching me dances to dance around while I was being shot. It was so cool. Jack, Margo, Marc and Scott all showed up. It was the first time I really felt like Tracy. The wig was amazing and William made my dress perfect … I wonder when the photos will come out … thank God I have photo approval! I can't wait until I'm in Times Square …

FEBRUARY 28, 2002, LOS ANGELES ☆ ☆ ☆ ☆ ☆

… I can't believe the movers come tomorrow. I can't believe I am moving back to New York to be on Broadway. I am so excited. I am flying first class! Shaiman called today and said the poster is up in Shubert Alley and said a gay crowd was standing around it … excited!!! … ☆☆☆

☆ APRIL 3, 2002, NEW YORK ☆

… "dance camp" is going well. I am so grateful I get to work alone with Jerry and the dance captain. I am going to be stressed when the cast of REAL dancers come in. Other than the damn mashed potato, I am doing well. Jerry is great. When something looks bad on me, he is quick to change it. I just learned NICEST KIDS IN TOWN. Everything hurts. Tomorrow I'll buy real dance shoes …

APRIL 29, 2002, NEW YORK ♡ ♡ ♡ ♡

William Ivey Long himself took me to Saks Fifth Avenue to buy me press clothes! This is crazy! We talked a lot about Tracy's wardrobe. I am so excited to see what he comes up with . . .

(oo) MAY 10, 2002, NEW YORK

I can't believe I forgot to bring Harvey flowers to rehearsal today for mother's Day! He'll never let me live this down! I need to write him a card. With all my stress about getting through rehearsal, and learning these dances, I keep forgetting to tell him that I would never have gotten this far without him. Because of our offstage connection, it makes our onstage stuff so easy. I have to make sure not to take him for granted . . . but what are mothers for . . . .

(oo) MAY 27, 2002, SEATTLE

I cannot do this. I have bronchitis and I am totally stressed out. The sicker I am, the more stressed I get. The more stressed I get, the sicker I feel. I had no idea how hard this was going to be. margo actually told me I was carrying a ten and a half million dollar show today! Harvey thinks I need therapy. No one understands. Previews start in 2 days. They sent me home from rehearsal. I am SO OVERWHELMED. This is all I ever wanted and now I feel like I am letting myself and everyone else down. I just want to be perfect. I know once I stop coughing I'll be fine but EVERYONE thinks I am having a nervous breakdown but I am just sick. Seattle is wet and cold. I wanna go home. (oo)

MAY 28, 2002, SEATTLE

marc and Scott came over tonight. They made me laugh so hard that I had to go to the hospital. While there, they found out I have been on the wrong medication and I am SO angry!!! See I am not having a breakdown, I AM REALLY SICK! . . . (oo)(oo)(oo)

♡ JULY 7, 2002, NEW YORK

. . . I went to theater for the first time today. I made Cade go with me. I was so nervous. I stood on the middle of the stage, unfortunately all the seats were covered with tarps for construction, and thought about Ethel merman performing on this stage. I can't wait for my family to see the show here. This is so unreal. The seats are so much closer, the front row will see right up my skirt and I'll definitely have to sing full-out in the finale! Went up the last row in the balcony and watched the crew load in our set. It still felt so intimate. This theatre is small, but perfect for our show . . . ♡

◎ ◎ ◎ ◎ AUGUST 16, 2002, NEW YORK ◎ ◎ ◎ ◎

Yesterday was a blur. I got to the theater at 2 and STILL was late for places! I was so overwhelmed by my dressing room. There were flowers everywhere! Anyone that walked in . . . walked out with a bouquet! At one point, I remember Judah (my boyfriend) and me standing on a chair, looking out the window that overlooked the red carpet. There were so many people, but of course we quickly spotted my panicked mother being escorted into the theater early to get water, use the bathroom, and calm down. I, on the other hand, was more excited than nervous. I had to keep reminding myself, this is it. This is all I ever wanted and no matter what the reviewers say, no one can take this night away from us. During GOOD MORNING BALTIMORE it all hit me when I sang the lyrics " . . . Today all my dreams will come true." It took every ounce of energy to keep from crying. Harvey and I promised we'd walk over to the party together, but he got ready before I did. Not only did Harvey not wait, but also the red carpet was gone when I came out the stage door. But thankfully they stopped traffic for me to cross the street to Roseland! The best part of the night was bumping back into Harvey on the street as I was walking home with my shoes in one hand and my boyfriend in the other. We all took some pictures, Harvey quoted the rave reviews . . . I finally slept . . . and slept and slept.

☆☆AUGUST 23 ,2002, NEW YORK

So many famous people have already come to the theater but tonight was ridiculous! In my very intimate dressing room stood (at once) Rob Reiner and family, Francis Ford Coppola and family, George Lucas and family!! Kay and I were standing pressed up between my costumes half in shock, half in awe but really there was just not enough room. The kicker was, as everyone was leaving, in walked Sissy Spacek . . .

☆ ☆ ☆ SEPTEMBER 16, 2002, NEW YORK ☆ ☆ ☆

Last week was insane! Yesterday I hosted Broadway on Broadway – does it get any better than that?! I was so proud of our cast . . . we were DEFINITELY the best (Friday we performed live on the Today show, Thursday I did an interview for People magazine for a feature they are doing on me, Wednesday I had 2 shows, Tuesday I did a photo shoot in the middle of Times Square for Glamour and next week we shoot Vogue magazine! what is going on?!)

h

"I'M A BIG GIRL NOW"

MOMS
STOP!

PENNY
STOP TELLING ME WHAT TO DO

MOMS
DON'T!

AMBER
DON'T TREAT ME LIKE A CHILD OF TWO

MOMS
NO!

TRACY
I KNOW THAT YOU WANT WHAT'S BEST

MOMS
PLEASE?

TRACY
BUT MOTHER, PLEASE,

ALL
GIVE IT A REST!!!

MOMS
STOP! DON'T! NO!

GIRLS
PLEASE!

MOMS
STOP! DON'T! NO!

GIRLS
PLEASE!

MOMS
STOP! DON'T! NO!

GIRLS
PLEASE!
MAMA, I'M A BIG GIRL NOW!

*(Scene shifts to the GIRLS'
bedroom vanities.)*

In one draft, we cut PENNY and PRUDY, so this song looked adrift without the visual one–two–three effect of the three eager girls and their stern moms.

TRACY

ONCE UPON A TIME
WHEN I WAS JUST A KID
YOU NEVER LET ME DO
JUST WHAT THE OLDER KIDS DID
BUT LOSE THAT LAUNDRY LIST
OF WHAT YOU WON'T ALLOW
'CAUSE MAMA,
I'M A BIG GIRL NOW

BACKUP

OOH'S . . .

. . . MAMA
I'M A BIG GIRL NOW

AMBER

ONCE UPON A TIME
I USED TO PLAY WITH TOYS
BUT NOW I'D RATHER PLAY AROUND
WITH TEENAGE BOYS
SO IF I GET A HICKEY,
PLEASE DON'T HAVE A COW
'CAUSE MAMA,
I'M A BIG GIRL NOW

OOH'S . . .

. . . MAMA
I'M A BIG GIRL NOW

PENNY

MA, I GOTTA TELL YOU
THAT WITHOUT A DOUBT
I GET MY BEST
DANCING LESSONS FROM YOU
YOU'RE THE ONE WHO TAUGHT ME
HOW TO TWIST AND SHOUT
BECAUSE YOU SHOUT NONSTOP
AND YOU'RE SO TWISTED TOO-OO
WA - OH - OH - OH - OH

OOH, OOH, OOH
OOH'S . . .

OOH, OOH, OOH
OOH'S . . .

TRACY

ONCE I USED TO FIDGET
'CAUSE I JUST SAT HOME

OOH'S . . .

AMBER

BUT NOW I'M JUST LIKE GIDGET
AND I GOTTA GET TO ROME!

OOH'S . . .

PENNY

SO SAY, ARRIVEDERCI!

OOH'S . . .

TRACY

TOODLE-LOO!

OOH'S . . .

"FEAR OF JOHN WATERS"
This verse replaced an earlier version of PENNY's complaint:

MA, YOU'RE ALWAYS TELLING ME
TO ACT MY AGE
WELL, THAT'S JUST WHAT
I'M TRYING TO DO
I'M A TEENAGE GIRL,
SO PLEASE UNLOCK THIS CAGE
I'M NOT ANNE FRANK
THIS ISN'T WORLD WAR TWO

In the movie Gidget Goes to Rome, she is wooed by James Darren—chastely, of course.

The vanities set

AMBER
AND CIAO!

ALL GIRLS
'CAUSE MAMA,
I'M A BIG GIRL NOW

BACKUP (cont'd)
OOH'S . . .

. . . MAMA
I'M A BIG GIRL NOW
OOH, OOH, OOH

ALL
STOP! DON'T! NO! PLEASE!
STOP! DON'T! NO! PLEASE!
STOP! DON'T! NO! PLEASE!
MAMA, I'M A BIG GIRL NOW

BACKUP
HEY MAMA, SAY MAMA

TRACY
ONCE UPON A TIME
I WAS A SHY YOUNG THING
COULD BARELY WALK AND TALK
SO MUCH AS DANCE AND SING
BUT LET ME HIT THAT STAGE,
I WANNA TAKE MY BOW
'CAUSE MAMA,
I'M A BIG GIRL NOW

OOH'S . . .

. . . MAMA
I'M A BIG GIRL NOW

AMBER	BACKUP (cont'd)
WA – OH – OH – OH – OH	
ONCE UPON A TIME	OOH'S . . .
I USED TO DRESS UP 'KEN'	
BUT NOW THAT I'M A WOMAN,	
I LIKE BIGGER MEN	
AND I DON'T NEED A BARBIE DOLL	
TO SHOW ME HOW	
'CAUSE MAMA,	. . . MAMA
I'M A BIG GIRL NOW	I'M A BIG GIRL NOW

ALL GIRLS

MA, YOU ALWAYS TAUGHT ME	OH, OH, OH, WA
WHAT WAS RIGHT FROM WRONG	OOH . . .
AND NOW I JUST WANNA GIVE IT A TRY	. . . GIVE IT A TRY
MAMA, I'VE BEEN IN THE NEST	WA, OOH'S . . .
FOR FAR TOO LONG	
SO PLEASE GIVE A PUSH	
AND MAMA WATCH ME FLY	AND MAMA WATCH ME FLY

AMBER

WATCH ME FLY
HEY, MAMA, SAY MAMA

PENNY

ONE DAY I WILL MEET A MAN	OOH'S . . .
YOU WON'T CONDEMN	

AMBER

AND WE WILL HAVE SOME KIDS	OOH'S . . .
AND YOU CAN TORTURE THEM	

TRACY

BUT LET ME BE A STAR
OOH'S . . .
BEFORE I TAKE THAT BOW

ALL GIRLS

'CAUSE MAMA,	MAMA
I'M A BIG GIRL NOW	I'M A BIG GIRL NOW

PENNY

OH – OH – OH

ALL GIRLS

MAMA,	MAMA
I'M A BIG GIRL NOW	BIG GIRL NOW

AMBER
HEY – HEY – HEY

BACKUP (cont'd)

ALL GIRLS
MAMA,
I'M A BIG GIRL NOW

MAMA,
I'M A BIG GIRL NOW

AMBER
OOH, SUCH A BIG, BIG GIRL!

OOH!

ALL GIRLS
I'M A BIG GIRL NOW . . .

ALL
STOP! DON'T! NO! PLEASE!
STOP! DON'T! NO! PLEASE!
STOP! DON'T! NO! PLEASE!
MAMA, I'M A BIG GIRL NOW!!!

GET TRACY TO THE CORNY COLLINS AUDITION

Without removing your pen from the page can you get Tracy to the omigosh all-important audition to be on the hottest teen dance show Baltimore?

Laurence Welk
Audition

Permanent
Detention

Stupid Bus
Crash

THE CORNY COLLINS AUDITION
Show

The Twilight
Zone

Unguarded
Picnic Basket

SOLUTION: Knowing Tracy, it's okay to just go right through the lines directly to the auditions! She's breaking down the walls! Go, Tracy, go!

CAN YOU MATCH THE CHARACTER TO HIS OR HER

SECRET VICE

! ?

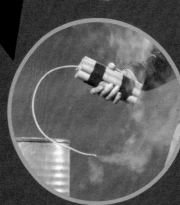

Act One
Scene 3

THE AUDITION

(The TV station. The COUNCIL MEMBERS and VELMA sit behind a long table.)

The very first draft of this scene was in rhymed beatnik verse, and everyone snapped their fingers in time. Arty, but it didn't work.

Libretto

48

LOU ANN

That's it, Mrs. Von Tussle. She was the last candidate.

VELMA

Really? That's all? Who would've guessed that Baltimore girls were all such skags? My, how this town has gone downhill since I was crowned Miss Baltimore Crabs.

(TRACY and PENNY enter, out of breath. The COUNCIL starts to break up.)

TRACY

Phew! I thought we'd never get here. Stupid bus crash!

PENNY

All my life I imagined what this place would look like. This isn't it.

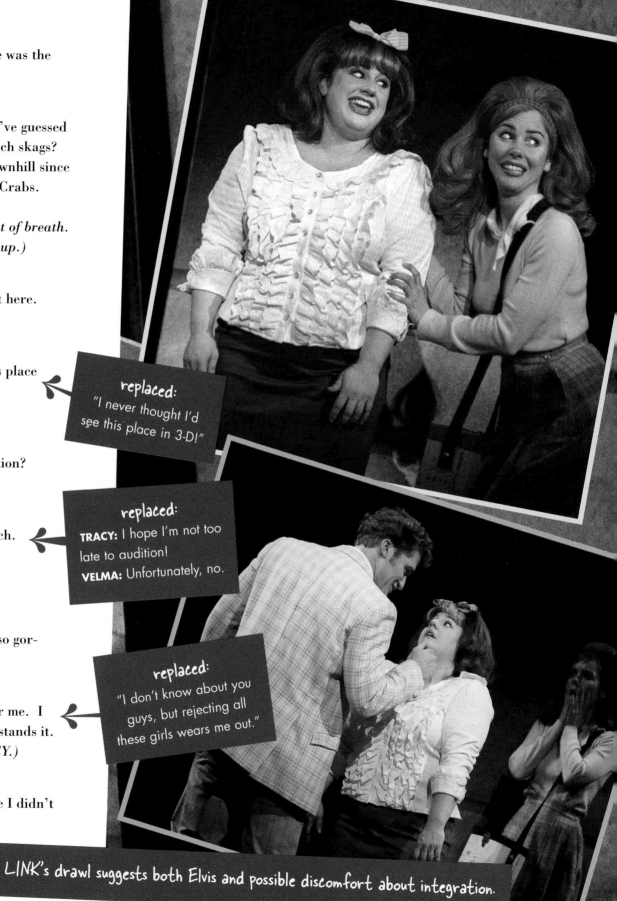

replaced:
"I never thought I'd see this place in 3-D!"

TRACY

(to VELMA)

Hi there. Am I too late to audition?

VELMA

(dismissing her)

Not too late, dear. Just too much.

replaced:
TRACY: I hope I'm not too late to audition!
VELMA: Unfortunately, no.

PENNY

Tracy. Look, it's Link!

TRACY

Link Larkin. So near, and yet so gorgeous.

LINK

I know, those girls were all over me. I don't know how Rock Hudson stands it. *(And he walks right into TRACY.)*

replaced:
"I don't know about you guys, but rejecting all these girls wears me out."

LINK

Excuse me, little darlin', I hope I didn't dent your do.
(ALL freeze except TRACY and PENNY.)

LINK's drawl suggests both Elvis and possible discomfort about integration.

"I CAN HEAR THE BELLS"

TRACY
I CAN HEAR THE BELLS

PENNY
Tracy, are you all right?

TRACY
DON'TCHA HEAR 'EM CHIME?

PENNY
I don't hear anything.

TRACY
CAN'TCHA HEAR MY HEARTBEAT
KEEPING PERFECT TIME?
AND ALL BECAUSE HE

TOUCHED ME
HE LOOKED AT ME AND STARED, YES HE
BUMPED ME
MY HEART WAS UNPREPARED WHEN HE
TAPPED ME
AND KNOCKED ME OFF MY FEET
ONE LITTLE TOUCH
NOW MY LIFE'S COMPLETE 'CAUSE WHEN HE

NUDGED ME
LOVE PUT ME IN A FIX, YES IT
HIT ME
JUST LIKE A TON OF BRICKS, YES MY
HEART BURST
NOW I KNOW WHAT LIFE'S ABOUT
ONE LITTLE TOUCH
AND LOVE KNOCKED ME OUT AND

BACKUP

I CAN HEAR THE BELLS   I CAN HEAR THE BELLS
MY HEAD IS SPINNING
I CAN HEAR THE BELLS   I CAN HEAR THE BELLS
SOMETHING'S BEGINNING
EVERYBODY SAYS
THAT A GIRL WHO LOOKS LIKE ME
CAN'T WIN HIS LOVE
WELL, JUST WAIT AND SEE

FEAR OF JOHN WATERS
Margo and her team asked for this kind of moment for TRACY. We're glad they did! On the other hand, Margo asked us to take out the "French kissing" lyric so that the song was 100% dreamy. I screamed, "I can't believe YOU are producing this show!" Luckily we laughed about this later, French kissed, and made up.

Marc and Scott taste-fully stop short of the "He Hit Me, But It Felt Like a Kiss" lyrics.

PENNY almost steals this scene, wandering through the fantasy spectacle without seeing any of it.

TRACY (cont'd)

'CAUSE I CAN HEAR THE BELLS	*BACKUP (cont'd)*
	I CAN HEAR THE BELLS

TRACY (cont'd)   **BACKUP** (cont'd)

'CAUSE I CAN HEAR THE BELLS   I CAN HEAR THE BELLS

JUST HEAR THEM CHIMING

I CAN HEAR THE BELLS   I CAN HEAR THE BELLS

MY TEMPERATURE'S CLIMBING

I CAN'T CONTAIN MY JOY

'CAUSE I FIN'LY FOUND THE BOY

I'VE BEEN MISSIN'

LISTEN, I CAN HEAR THE BELLS

                                AH'S . . .

ROUND ONE   ROUND ONE

HE'LL ASK ME ON A DATE AND THEN

ROUND TWO   ROUND TWO

I'LL PRIMP, BUT WON'T BE LATE BECAUSE

ROUND THREE'S   ROUND THREE

WHEN WE KISS INSIDE HIS CAR

WON'T GO ALL THE WAY

BUT I'LL GO PRETTY FAR THEN,

ROUND FOUR   ROUND FOUR

HE'LL ASK ME FOR MY HAND AND THEN

ROUND FIVE   ROUND FIVE

WE'LL BOOK THE WEDDING BAND SO BY

ROUND SIX   ROUND SIX

AMBER, MUCH TO YOUR SURPRISE

THIS HEAVYWEIGHT CHAMPION

TAKES THE PRIZE AND   TAKES THE PRIZE AND

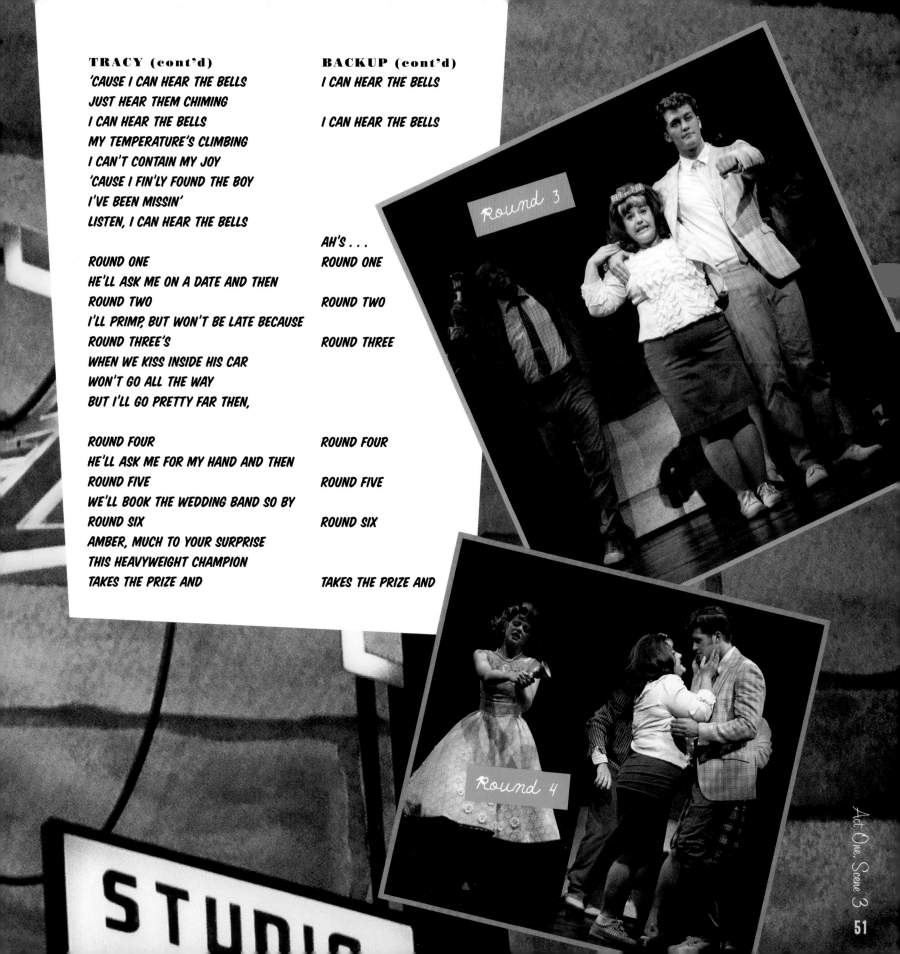

Round 3

Round 4

Because CORNY, as the Drunken Minister, carries a Veuve Clicquot bottle in this number, the company received some complimentary bottles of the champagne for opening night.

Early-'60s pop songs are full of dead teenagers.

TRACY (cont'd)	BACKUP (cont'd)
I CAN HEAR THE BELLS	I CAN HEAR THE BELLS
MY EARS ARE RINGING	
I CAN HEAR THE BELLS	I CAN HEAR THE BELLS
THE BRIDESMAIDS ARE SINGING	
EVERYBODY SAYS	AH'S . . .
THAT A GUY WHO'S SUCH A GEM	
WON'T LOOK MY WAY	
BUT THE LAUGH'S ON THEM 'CAUSE	
I CAN HEAR THE BELLS	I CAN HEAR THE BELLS
MY FATHER WILL SMILE	
I CAN HEAR THE BELLS	I CAN HEAR THE BELLS
AS HE WALKS ME DOWN THE AISLE	
MY MOTHER STARTS TO CRY	
BUT I CAN'T SEE 'CAUSE LINK AND I	
ARE FRENCH KISSIN'	
LISTEN, I CAN HEAR THE BELLS	AH . . . AH . . . AH . . . AH . . .
I CAN HEAR THE BELLS	I CAN HEAR THE BELLS
MY HEAD IS REELING	
I CAN HEAR THE BELLS	I CAN HEAR THE BELLS
I CAN'T STOP THE PEALING	
EVERYBODY WARNS	AH . . .
THAT HE WON'T LIKE WHAT HE'LL SEE	AH . . .
BUT I KNOW THAT HE'LL LOOK	AH . . . AH
INSIDE OF ME, YEAH	INSIDE OF ME, YEAH
I CAN HEAR THE BELLS	I CAN HEAR THE BELLS
TODAY'S JUST THE START 'CAUSE	
I CAN HEAR THE BELLS	I CAN HEAR THE BELLS
AND 'TIL DEATH DO US PART	
AND EVEN WHEN WE DIE	OO . . . OO . . .
WE'LL LOOK DOWN FROM UP ABOVE	OO . . . OO . . .
REMEMBERING THE NIGHT	OO . . . OO . . .
THAT WE TWO FELL IN LOVE	. . . TWO FELL IN LOVE
WE BOTH WILL SHARE A TEAR	
AND HE'LL WHISPER AS WE'RE REMINISCIN'	. . . 'NISCIN'
LISTEN!	

TRACY (cont'd)	BACKUP (cont'd)
I CAN HEAR THE BELLS	*SHE CAN HEAR THE BELLS*
I CAN HEAR THE BELLS	*SHE CAN HEAR THE BELLS*
I CAN HEAR THE BELLS	*BONG*
	BONG
	BONG
	BONG

(The song ends. The COUNCILETTES, led by AMBER, interrogate TRACY.)

AMBER

And what are you doing here?

TRACY

I came to audition for Corny. My name is Tracy Turnblad.
And, like you, I go to Patterson Park High . . .

LOU ANN

I've seen you.

AMBER

Who could miss her? Aren't you usually in detention about now?

TRACY

I cut school to come down here. Isn't that too cool? I'm a little nervous, can
I start over? I assure you I'll calm down, right after I have a heart attack!!
(MUSIC in)
Well, I brought my own 45s, so if you put 'em on, I'll show you my stuff!

LOU ANN

Haven't you already shown us enough?
(The COUNCILETTES snicker.)

The TRACY–AMBER battle officially begins here.

A real Baltimore high school.

CUT
"I've seen you . . . around!"

The small vinyl records, not the pistols.

Originally, there was no song here. Then several different songs variously filled this spot, including a cha-cha called "The Status Quo." VELMA's devious, but Latin may be too smart for her.

"(THE LEGEND OF) MISS BALTIMORE CRABS"

VELMA
OH MY GOD
HOW TIMES HAVE CHANGED
THIS GIRL'S EITHER BLIND
OR COMPLETELY DERANGED
AH, BUT TIME SEEMED TO HALT
WHEN I WAS "MISS BALTIMORE CRABS"

TRACY
It's been my childhood dream to dance on this show!

AMBER
Well, maybe you oughta go back to sleep!

VELMA
CHILDHOOD DREAMS
FOR ME WERE CRACKED
WHEN THAT DAMN SHIRLEY TEMPLE
STOLE MY FRICKIN' ACT
BUT THE CROWN'S IN THE VAULT
FROM WHEN I WON "MISS BALTIMORE CRABS"
THOSE POOR RUNNER-UPS
MIGHT STILL HOLD SOME GRUDGES
THEY PADDED THEIR 'CUPS'
BUT I SCREWED THE JUDGES
THOSE BROADS THOUGHT THEY'D WIN
IF A PLATE THEY WOULD SPIN IN THEIR DANCE
HA! NOT A CHANCE!

CAUSE I HIT THE STAGE
BATONS ABLAZE
WHILE SINGING AIDA
AND PREPARING CHEESE SOUFFLES!
BUT THAT TRIPLE SOMERSAULT
WAS HOW I CLINCHED "MISS BALTIMORE CRABS"!
(to the COUNCILETTES)
FIRE AWAY, GIRLS!

TAMMY
YOU'RE TOO WIDE FROM THE BACK

AMBER
HONEY, LOOK AT HER FRONT!

Act One, Scene 3

57

VELMA
*WAIT, ARE WE ON "CANDID CAMERA"?
OK, WHERE IS ALLEN FUNT?*

AMBER
DO YOU DANCE LIKE YOU DRESS?

LINK
GIRLS, THERE'S NO NEED TO BE CRUEL!

The first sign that LINK's a good guy.

VELMA
WOULD YOU SWIM IN AN INTEGRATED POOL?
(The MUSIC stops dead and the COUNCIL gasps in shock.)

TRACY
Sure I would. I'm all for integration. It's the New Frontier!

VELMA
Not in Baltimore it isn't.

TRACY
Um, where's Corny? I'd love to dance for him.

VELMA
I'm the producer and may I be frank?
(MUSIC back in, ominously building, building)

*FIRST IMPRESSIONS CAN BE TOUGH
AND WHEN I SAW YOU, I KNEW IT
IF YOUR SIZE WEREN'T ENOUGH
THAT LAST ANSWER JUST BLEW IT!*

*AND SO, MY DEAR, SO SHORT AND STOUT
YOU'LL NEVER BE "IN"*

VELMA & COUNCIL MEMBERS
SO WE'RE KICKING YOU OUT!

VELMA
*WITH YOUR FORM AND YOUR FACE
WELL, IT ISN'T YOUR FAULT
YOU'RE JUST DOWN WITH A CASE OF "MISS . . .*

VELMA & THE COUNCIL MEMBERS
BALTIMORE . . .

VELMA
. . . CRABS!"

COUNCIL QUESTIONS

Who's your favorite Hollywood star?
What's your favorite TV show?
What's your favorite slow dance?
What's your favorite fast dance?
What are your ambitions?
What's your favorite food?
What are your hobbies?
What's your favorite pastime?
Are you now going or have you ever gone steady?
Exactly how many sweaters do you have?
As a Negro can you relate to Lesley Gore's music?
Would you do a pimple cream commercial on camera if Corny asked you?
Would you swim in an integrated swimming pool??
Can Liz Taylor marry again?

VELMA

AM I ON CANDID CAMERA?
THIS HAS GOT TO BE A JOKE!
PLEASE SAY IT'S APRIL FOOL'S DAY
OR I MIGHT JUST HAVE A STROKE!

THIS GIRL DESERVES OUR PITY
THAT'S FOR SURE, SO PASS THE HAT
OH, BUT NO ONE ON THIS TV SHOW
WILL EVER LOOK LIKE THAT!

WHEN I WAS JUST A LITTLE GIRL
MY MOTHER SET ME STRAIGHT
SHE TAUGHT ME WHAT TO SAY
AND HOW TO DRESS AND WHO TO HATE

I'M JUST MY MOTHER'S DAUGHTER
SO I KNEW IN NO TIME FLAT
THAT NOBODY ON THIS TV SHOW
WILL EVER LOOK LIKE THAT!

SHE'S SHORT, SHE'S STOUT,
BEHIND THOSE CHEEKS IT'S NOT A PRETTY FACE
SHE'S NOT WHAT VELMA'S PUBLIC WANTS TO SEE

MUST ADMIT THIS WORLD
WOULD BE A MUCH MORE LOVELY PLACE
IF EVERYBODY IN IT LOOKED LIKE ME!
WHY IS IT UP TO MOI TO TEACH
THE LOWLIFE PUBLIC WHAT IT NEEDS?
I GUESS IT'S JUST MY CALLING
TO HELP GOD PLUCK OUT THE WEEDS

SO, EVEN IF ALL BALTIMORE
GETS STRUCK BLIND AS A BAT
BROTHER, NO ONE ON MY TV SHOW
WILL EVER LOOK LIKE THAT!

WELL, I'M AFRAID YOUR TIME IS UP
YOUR CHANCE TO SHINE IS GONE
BUT HERE'S SOME MOTHERLY ADVICE
FOR YOU TO CHEW UPON

DEAR, MAY I SUGGEST SOME FAR LESS
GLAM'ROUS DREAM WHICH TO PURSUE . . .
BECAUSE NO ONE ON THIS TV SHOW

A FEW GIRLS JOIN IN
NO ONE ON THIS TV SHOW

MORE GIRLS JOIN IN
NO ONE ON THIS TV SHOW

ALL GIRLS
WILL EV . . . ER . . .
LOOK . . . LIKE . . .

VELMA
. . . YOU!

CUT ✂

The audience was so in love with TRACY after "I Can Hear The Bells," they didn't want to see her attacked. In the end we decided to tailor the song to Linda Hart's strength as VELMA. The song was written before previews began in New York.

VELMA

You're free to go.

TRACY

Uh, thank you?

PENNY

I could tell they secretly liked you.
(LITTLE INEZ runs on.)

LITTLE INEZ

Hello, ma'am, may I please audition?

VELMA

Of course not!

BUT YOU CAN BOW AND EXALT
'CAUSE I AM "MISS BALTIMORE . . .

VELMA & COUNCIL MEMBERS

. . . CRABS"

replaced:
"Gee, that went well!"
and countless others.

replaced:
LITTLE INEZ: I hope I'm
not too late to audition!
VELMA: Fortunately, yes.

It's still a tough spot
for a joke because
LITTLE INEZ is
entering during it.

**COMEDY
THEORY:**
Nobody on
stage moves while a
joke is being delivered.

(The scene shifts as TRACY and LITTLE INEZ step down-stage and pass one other.)

TRACY & LITTLE INEZ
I KNOW EVERY STEP
I KNOW EVERY SONG
I KNOW THERE'S A PLACE WHERE I BELONG . . .

TRACY
(She reaches the mirror.)
Why do they have to be so mean? "You're short, you're stout, you're not Council material." I wear the latest fashions, I keep up with all the styles. I'm teasing my hair as high as I can!
(She sprays her hair with hairspray.)
Will they give me a chance? Encouragement? Appreciation? No.

Their unwitting duet points up for the first time that the battle for civil rights and for acceptance for anyone are the same battle.

There was a scene that followed this set in the Har-De-Har Hut, where WILBUR tried to cheer up the discouraged TRACY with a song. The first take was called "It Doesn't Get Better Than This," which was replaced by "Positivity," a satirical version of a Disney-esque "cheer up" song. We found the scene wasn't necessary, as charming as the moment was.

INSPIRATION FOR WILBUR'S SONG:
CLASSIC LIFE PHILOSOPHY SONGS
"Pick Yourself Up"
"High Hopes"
"On the Sunny Side of the Street"
"Keep Your Sunny Side Up"
"When You're Smiling"
"Life Is Just a Bowl of Cherries"
"The Best Things in Life Are Free"
"Smile"
"You're Nobody till Somebody Loves You"
"Make Someone Happy"

OH, WHEN YOU'RE BORN A TURNBLAD
THERE'S NO NEED TO FROWN MORE
FOR THERE'S MAGIC INSIDE OF YOUR GENES
CAUSE A TURNBLAD HAS
TAKE A SPRINKLING OF FAITH
WHEN ALL THE OTHERS LOSE
PLUS A SMIDGEON OF HOPE
LET ME
WHICH I'LL ILLUSTRATE NOW WITH
HIS TORICAL SCENES
WITH THESE HEARTWARMING SCENES

EVERY TURNBLAD HAS BEEN AT END OF HIS ROPE
BUT THE END ALWAYS JUSTIFIES THE MEANS

CAUSE WHEN TRAGEDY FALLS
WELL THEN A TURNBLAD HAS HOPE ITS A
YOUR GRANI THAT THE ENDING JUST AN END
WILL JUSTIFY THE MEANS END ALWAYS JUSTIFIES THE MEANS

YOUR
OH GRANDMA WAS UGLY
WITH WARTS ON HER NOSE/CHIN
BUT NOTHING COMPARED
TO HER SIAMESE TWIN
THE WORLD WATCHED IN SHOCK AWE
RACED TO RE
AS THEY WALKED DOWN THE STREET
FOR THEY'D WIN EVERY RACE
USING MULTIPLE FEET

THEY NEVER WERE LONELY
THEY NEVER WERE DOWN
AND THEY REALLY CLEANED UP
WHEN THE CIRCUS HIT TOWN
FOR THE ROUGH HER MARE
WHEN THE CIRCUS HIT TOWN

WHEN DAY IS DONE
THEY FOUND OUT THAT / MARRIAGE IS FUN
THEIR MEN FOUND THAT
2 HEADS ARE BETTER THAN ONE
ON YOUR WEDDING NIGHT

2

REMEMBER THE STRIPPER
WHO LIVED DOWN THE HALL
HER DAY DREAMS WERE BIG
BUT HER HOO-HA'S WERE SMALL

MY UNCLE WORE RAINCOATS
THOUGH IT NEVER RAINED
HE SHOWED OFF THE LINING
'TILL SOMEONE COMPLAINED

MY UNCLE WAS FUNNY

HE LOVED JUDY GARLAND
AND DRESSED LIKE HER TOO
                    A
ONE NIGHT AT THE PRIZE FIGHT
HE CAUSED QUITE A BRAWL
NOW HE LOVES IT IN JAIL
CAUSE HE'S "BELL OF THE BALL"

3

CAUSE WITH POSITIVITY
THEY JUST HAD FUN
AND THEIR DATES FOUND
THAT TWO HEADS ARE BETTER THAN ONE

CAUSE WITH POSITIVITY
THEY NEVER SPLIT
AND ON HALLOWEEN NIGHT
THEY WERE REALLY A HIT!

CAUSE WITH POSITIVITY
THEY COULD CARE LESS
THOUGH WHEN ONLY ONE DIED
IT WAS REALLY A MESS

CAUSE WITH POSITIVITY
THEY MADE THEIR POINT
BUT THOUGH WHEN ONLY ONE DIED
SHE SURE STUNK UP THE JOINT!

THEY FOUND A MATE
(BECAUSE TWO HEADS ARE BETTER
    THAN ONE ON A DATE!

THEY MADE A PACT / AND IT'S A FACT
(THAT) THEY MARRIED THE BAND
NOT TO SPLIT UP THE ACT

4

I ONCE
SO, I DREAMED INVENTIONS   WHEN I WAS A KID
                    I WOULD DREAM ALL THE DAY
WOULD
'TILL I GOT YOUR MOM
IN THE FAMILY WAY

                        GOODBYE TO THE NOBEL
I FEARED THAT MY HOPES   IES   + PULITER PRIZE
FOR THE FUTURE ____
BUT MY DREAMS ALL CAME TRUE
WHEN I LOOKED IN YOUR EYES

AND THAT'S
POS...... , POS .....

POS

I ONCE DREAMED   DREAMED OF
OF GLORY   I LOVED MY INVENTIONS
FROM PAPER-   AND TINKERED ALL DAY
        MACHE

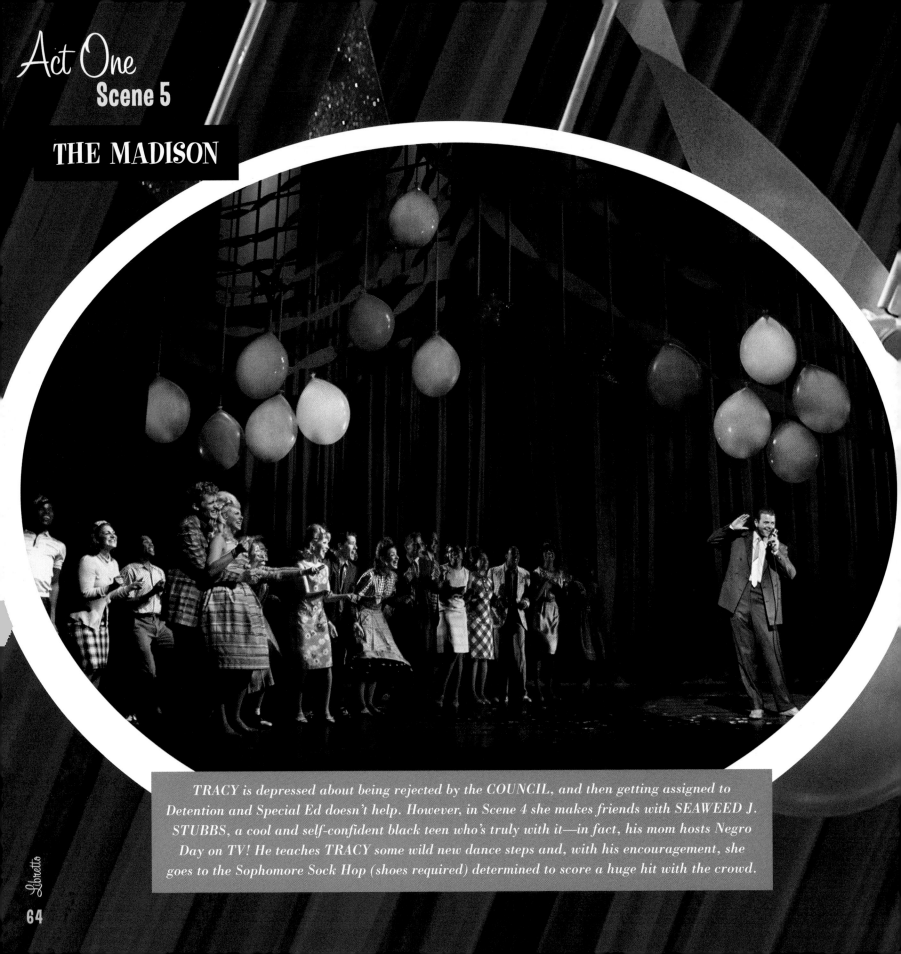

Act One
Scene 5

THE MADISON

TRACY is depressed about being rejected by the COUNCIL, and then getting assigned to Detention and Special Ed doesn't help. However, in Scene 4 she makes friends with SEAWEED J. STUBBS, a cool and self-confident black teen who's truly with it—in fact, his mom hosts Negro Day on TV! He teaches TRACY some wild new dance steps and, with his encouragement, she goes to the Sophomore Sock Hop (shoes required) determined to score a huge hit with the crowd.

CORNY

Hey, there, sophomores and sophomores at heart. I'm honored to be your guest DJ here at PPHS. So with no further a do-do, let's do-do some dancing. It's the hottest dance around and it was born right here in Baltimore. What's it called kids?

STUDENTS

The Madison!

CORNY

And where'd you see it first?

STUDENTS

The Corny Collins Show!

CORNY

Let's form two big strong lines—it's Madison time! Go! *(The KIDS form lines and dance.)*

STUDENTS
BABY DON'T SLEEP
BABY DON'T EAT
BABY JUST LIKES TO DO THE BOINK-BOINK
(TRACY enters with SEAWEED.)

STUDENTS *(under dialogue)*
BABY DON'T CALL
BABY WON'T MEET
BABY JUST LIKES TO DO THE BOINK-BOINK

I TRY TO LIE DOWN
BUT SHE'S ALWAYS ON HER FEET
TO DO THE BOINK-BOINK

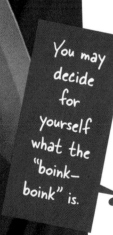

You may decide for yourself what the "boink-boink" is.

✂ CUT
Student in crowd:
"Hey, Corny! Show us your cob!"

In the movie, "The Madison" has no lyrics. We dreamed these up.

TRACY

Hurry, Seaweed, the dance has already started!

SEAWEED

Alright, but remember, you gotta dance with your crowd and I gotta dance with mine.

Additional lyrics for "The Madison"

"BOINK-BOINK"

SHE DON'T RUN
SHE DON'T WALK
BABY JUST LIKES TO DO
THE BOINK-BOINK

SHE DON'T KISS
SHE DON'T TALK
BABY JUST LIKES TO DO
THE BOINK-BOINK

I TAKE HER TO CLUBS AND RESTAURANTS
BUT ALL SHE EVER WANTS
TO DO IS BOINK-BOINK

TRACY

Oh look, it's the Madison, my favorite!

SEAWEED

You keep your eye on Corny. This could be your big chance.

TRACY

Then you better keep an eye on me.

Shades of Pygmalion?

CORNY

Now when I say, "Hit it," show me a big, bad Baltimore
Box. . . . Hit it!
(The KIDS do the dance.)
(TRACY insinuates herself in.)

High–school blacks and whites in the '60s attended the same dances, but a rope down the middle of the floor separated them.

STUDENTS

BOINK, BOINK

LITTLE INEZ

How come we always have to dance in the back?

SEAWEED

I don't know. There's them and there's us.
That's just the way it is.

The simple truth: Jack O'Brien's line.

CORNY

When I say, "Hit it," take it to the basket like
Wilt the Stilt. . . . Hit it!
(to AMBER)
Amber, who's your friend? She's like a breath of fresh,
mountain air.

AMBER

You got the mountain part right. Oink-oink.

CORNY

Now when I say, "Hit it," let's take a drive down Druid
Hill. . . . Hit it! Hang a right. . . . Feed the monkey. . . .
He's in the back seat.
(ALL dance)

STUDENTS

BOINK, BOINK

A real street, though Baltimorons pronounce it "Drood." John Waters told us about it.

LINK

(to TRACY)
Hey, little darlin'. Haven't we met somewhere?

The Madison

start 1. 2. clap! 3. 4. 5. touch! 6.

If Tracy can learn it, so can you!

The Baltimore Box

start 1. 2. 3. 4.

THE MADISON

I learned the Madison from Linda Snider and her husband Gene, who met dancing on The Buddy Deane Show in Baltimore.

The Madison is a simple line dance that was all the rage in the '60s. Everyone stands in a line and does the basic step until the caller calls out a new step. When he or she says, "Hit it!" everyone dances the new step and then goes back to the basic Madison.

My job was to take that simple line dance and make it interesting to watch on stage. The story needed to continue through the dance and eventually land Tracy as the newest Council Member in The Corny Collins Show.

Early on, I realized staying in one line on stage would make the dance stagnant. So I shuffled the lines when needed, allowing different characters to be downstage delivering their lines as the Madison was being called out by Corny Collins.

When Corny sees Tracy dance, we spin into fantasy and then return to the show. Tracy demonstrates her step, "Peyton Place after Midnight," which she learned from her friend Seaweed, and wins a place on the show. Hit it!

—Jerry Mitchell

TRACY

Link Larkin actually spoke to me. I'll never wash this ear again.

Again, this joke is Jack O'Brien's. Collaboration is a rich experience, and easier than real work.

CORNY

When I say, "Hit it," let's make like Jackie Gleason—hommina, hommina, hommina. . . . Hit it!
(ALL start step.)

ALL

And away we go!

TRACY

Hi, Corny!

CORNY

Hey, cupcake. What's your name?

TRACY

(as she does the "My Name Is" step)
I'm Tracy Turnblad.

CORNY

What else have you got hiding in those Buster Browns?

These were budget kids' shoes.

TRACY

Well, here's one I picked up in detention. It's called "Peyton Place after Midnight." I use it to attract the opposite sex.

SEAWEED

Hey, hey, hey! Check her out, everybody!
(TRACY does the step as the KIDS join in.)

Pretty generous, since it's his step.

LINK

That girl's as free as the wind.

This is why LINK will love TRACY.

AMBER

Everybody stop liking her!!!!

CORNY

OK, everybody, let's take it home. Crazy!
(The KIDS do the Madison.)
And that, Baltimorians, is how we do the Madison.

We try to keep the fact that CORNY's put TRACY on his show a surprise until Scene 6.

Hair Hoppery

Paul Huntley, Wig Designer

When I was asked to design and make the wigs for *Hairspray* my reaction was, "Oh dear, spray . . . teasing . . . beehives . . . ugly!" My reputation was natural, natural, natural. But with inspiration from the John Waters movie and William Ivey Long's glorious costumes, how could I say no? And it proved to be a joyous task. John Waters gave me the key—just think Versailles on speed. And to quote that immortal hair creed of the 1960s: The higher the hair the nearer to god. I think I may have just achieved this!

Try on the wigs! Find a photo with your face the size of this lilac oval, color copy these wigs, cut them out, and try them on!

SUCCESS

CORNY *boldly puts* TRACY *on the show—and she's an instant hit! Her folks at home are shocked and then delighted, and they're flooded with congratulatory phone calls. Then* LINK *even sings a song to* TRACY *right on the air!*

CORNY

Link Larkin, our own budding Elvis, will now sing to the equally blooming Tracy Turnblad his version of this week's Top 40 hit, "It Takes Two."

AMBER

Mother!

"IT TAKES TWO"

LOST TO HISTORY:
In the first draft, he was a budding Gene Pitney, but no one knew who that was.

BACKUP

OOH OO OO OO OO OOH
OOH OO OO OO
IT TA-AKES TWO
OOH OO OO OO OO OO
OOH DOO DOO WOP!

LINK

THEY SAY IT'S A MAN'S WORLD
WELL, THAT CANNOT BE DENIED
BUT WHAT GOOD'S A MAN'S WORLD
WITHOUT A WOMAN BY HIS SIDE
AND SO I WILL WAIT
UNTIL THAT MOMENT YOU DECIDE

THAT I'M YOUR MAN	. . . I'M YOUR MAN
AND YOU'RE MY GIRL	AND YOU'RE MY GIRL
THAT I'M THE SEA	. . . I'M THE SEA
AND YOU'RE THE PEARL	AND YOU'RE THE PEARL
IT TAKES TWO BABY,	IT TAKES TWO - OO - OO
IT TAKES TWO	IT TAKES TWO - OO
	DOO DOO WOP

A KING AIN'T A KING	OOH
WITHOUT THE POW'R BEHIND THE THRONE	OOH
A PRINCE IS A PAUPER, BABE	OOH
WITHOUT A CHICK TO CALL HIS OWN	OOH
SO PLEASE DARLING CHOOSE ME	AAH - AAH
I DON'T WANNA RULE ALONE	AAH - AAH

TELL ME I'M YOUR KING	. . . I'M YOUR KING
AND YOU'RE MY QUEEN	AND YOU'RE MY QUEEN
THAT NO ONE ELSE	THAT NO ONE ELSE
CAN COME BETWEEN	CAN COME BETWEEN
IT TAKES TWO BABY,	IT TAKES TWO - OO - OO
IT TAKES TWO	IT TAKES TWO - OO
	OO-DON'TCHA KNOW

LINK

LANCELOT HAD GUINEVERE
MRS. CLAUS HAS OLD ST. NICK
ROMEO HAD JULIET
AND LIZ, SHE HAS HER DICK
THEY SAY IT TAKES TWO TO TANGO
BUT THAT TANGO'S CHILD'S PLAY
SO TAKE ME TO THE DANCE FLOOR

AND WE'LL TWIST THE NIGHT AWAY

JUST LIKE FRANKIE AVALON
HAS HIS FAVORITE MOUSEKETEER
I DREAM OF A LOVER, BABE
TO SAY THE THINGS I LONG TO HEAR
SO COME CLOSER BABY,
OH AND WHISPER IN MY EAR

TRACY
YEAH . . .

BACKUP

HOOT, HOOT, HOOT, HOOT
OW-OOT , HOOT, HOOT, HOO-OO
HOOT, HOOT, HOOT, HOOT
OW-OOT, HOOT, HOOT, HOO-OO
HOOT, HOOT, HOOT, HOOT
OW-OOT, AAH AAH AAH OOH
AAH AAH AAH AAH

AAH AAH AAH AAH

OOH
OOH WA - OOH WA
OOH - OO - OO - OO - OOH
. . . WOP WA
OOH - OOO
OOO - AAH

Libretto

LINK
THAT YOU'RE MY GIRL
AND I'M YOUR BOY

THAT YOU'RE MY PRIDE

AND I'M YOUR JOY
THAT I'M THE SAND
AND YOU'RE THE TIDE
I'LL BE THE GROOM
IF YOU'LL BE MY BRIDE
IT TAKES TWO BABY,
IT TAKES TWO
IT TAKES TWO BABY,

LINK & TRACY
IT TAKES TWO

TRACY & GUYS
. . . I'M YOUR GIRL
. . . YOU'RE MY BOY

. . . YOU'RE MY PRIDE

. . . I'M YOUR JOY
. . . I'M THE SAND
. . . YOU'RE THE TIDE
. . . BE THE GROOM
. . . BE MY BRIDE
IT TAKES TWO-00-00-00
IT TAKES TWO-00-00-00
AAH - AAH

GUYS
. . . TWO-00-00-00-00
00 - 00 - 00 - OOH

TRACY is now a big TV success, but the sponsor, MR. SPRITZER, is uneasy about her liberal attitudes, and VELMA is furious that CORNY has gone over her head in bringing in TRACY. "It's time we put kids on the show who look like the kids who watch the show!" CORNY declares, but crazy VELMA vows vengeance on him and TRACY.

Since BRENDA ran off nauseated, BRAD is left alone to grieve. CORNY consoles him.

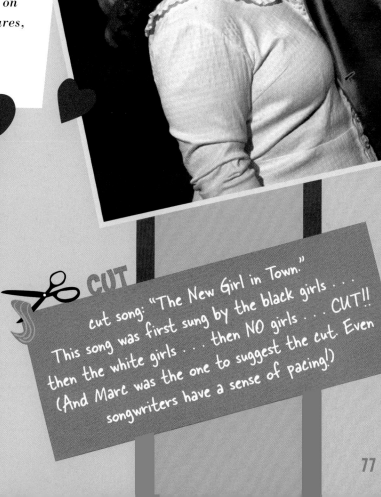

CUT

cut song: "The New Girl in Town."
This song was first sung by the black girls . . .
then the white girls . . . then NO girls . . . CUT!!
(And Marc was the one to suggest the cut. Even songwriters have a sense of pacing!)

Tracy and Edna's Journey as Reflected in Their Clothing

William Ivey Long, Costume Designer

The *Hairspray* costume adventure traces Tracy Turnblad's Cinderella transformation from blue-collar couch potato at her parents' laundry to Princess of the Prom.

Many friends help Tracy along the Yellow Brick Fashion Road: her loving, supportive parents (themselves sartorial disasters); her best friend, Penny; her new friend, the electric Seaweed (the King of Pop and Op Art); and ultimately the Pygmalion, Mr. Pinky. I myself have channeled Mr. Pinky.

Tracy's first at-home and at-school outfits are short, tight skirts topped off with the infamous "Angel Blouse" John Waters swears all girls wore to torment their horrified parents— all flounces of ruffles down the front, resulting in the pregnant-teenager look.

On the other hand, Edna Turnblad does not aspire to become a fashion icon. In fact, she doesn't even know she is missing out on anything. In "Welcome to the '60s," Mr. Pinky transforms her from housefrau into his version of Glorious Pucci: swirly '60s prints in silk and chiffon garnished with ostrich feathers, a newly dyed and set coiffeur, and matching high-heeled pumps.

Edna's next "Chicken and Waffles" two-piece suit is inspired by the looks Oleg Cassini created for First Lady Jacqueline Kennedy. The difference: a *horror vacui* sensibility allowing no stretch of fabric to remain unembellished, no hem unflounced or unruffled—all whipped cream and flourish.

John Waters instructed me about the other-side-of-the-tracks Von Tussles' wardrobe mantra—whenever they went shopping at the grocery store, they dressed as if going to a ball at Versailles. This image is made manifest in the "Can't Stop the Beat" finale with Velma and Amber as Marie Antoinette

wannabes morphed through Balenciaga into sublime Tammy Fae Baker.

Throughout the clothing journey of Tracy and Edna, each and every detail is important—these are real clothes, not costumes. Mr. Pinky means everything he says. By contrast, David Rockwell's scenery is suggestive—explosions of attitude and crystallized abstractions of the 1960s, as if in a ballet. There are only one door and one doorknob in the whole show. In the world of the clothes, everything is doorknobs. And light switches. Every part of every piece of clothing is a wearable choice. Every choice tells a story. And what a story.

"good morning Baltimore"

in jail "Without Love"

"Can't Stop the Beat"

"Timeless to Me"

"Welcome to
the 60's"

"Edna" "Chicken & Waffles"
Harvey Fierstein "Hairspray"

"Welcome to
the 60's"

"Edna": Finale Back View
Harvey Fierstein "Hairspray"

Act One Scene 7

Libretto

(The TURNBLAD home. EDNA is frazzled from hours on the phone.)

EDNA

(into the phone)

Yes. Thank you so much! . . . I'm sure Tracy appreciates your vote for Miss Teenage Hairspray. Yes! And she loves you, too. Very much. Whoever you are. Goodbye!

(the phone rings again)

This is crazy.

(answering)

Hello? What am I wearing? A housecoat, scuffies, and Supp-Hose®. What are you wearing? Hello? Hello?

(Puzzled, she hangs up.)

TRACY

(bursting in excitedly)

Mama, did you see, did you see me?

EDNA

Of course I did. It was on television. I had to. The phone's been ringing like we was a telethon. To think, the fruit of my womb, a beloved TV icon.

TRACY

So you're not mad?

EDNA

Mad? How could I be mad? You're famous! If you'd only told me you was going to get on the show I never would have said you couldn't. But sit. . . . Tell me, is fame all you thought it would be? Are you happy, honey?

TRACY

Yes, Mama. And I think I'm in love.

EDNA

I know. I've been following. But you and I are going to have to have a talk about crooners. You can learn a lot from the mistakes of Miss Debbie Reynolds.

(The telephone rings.)

And there it goes again.

TRACY

(answering the phone)

Hello? Yes, this is Tracy Turnblad. Hello, Mr. Pinky.

EDNA

(in an excited whisper)

Mr. Pinky? THE Mr. Pinky? As in "MR. PINKY'S HEFTY HIDEAWAY— QUALITY CLOTHES FOR QUANTITY GALS"? That Mr. Pinky?

Supp-Hose® offered support, presumably for older ladies.

A joke of the 1970s: "Bill Cosby's not black, he's famous!"

"QUALITY CLOTHES FOR QUANTITY GALS" replaced: "WHERE BOUNTIFUL IS BEAUTIFUL!"

81

TRACY

You want to hire me as your exclusive spokesgirl and fashion effigy?
(to EDNA)
What's an effigy?
(back on the phone)
That's very flattering, but I'm afraid all business must go through my agent. . . . It would be our pleasure. We'll be right over, Mr. Pinky. Goodbye!
(TRACY hangs up the phone.)

EDNA

An agent! I don't know any agents. How about a nice bail bondsman?

TRACY

Mother, put that thing down. I'm taking my new agent to the Hefty Hideaway and then out on the town.

EDNA

Who? Me? Tracy Turnblad, fame has gone to your head and left you wacky. You need a top-shelf professional. Who handled the Gabor sisters? Well, who didn't?

TRACY

Mama, there's a great big world out there I know nothing about. When things get rough, a girl needs her mother.

EDNA

Hun, I'll be right beside you, if that's what you want. And together we'll claw your way to the top. But can't we do it over the phone? I haven't been out of this apartment since Mamie Eisenhower rolled her hose and bobbed her bangs.

"WELCOME TO THE '60S"

TRACY
HEY MAMA HEY MAMA, LOOK AROUND
EVERYBODY'S GROOVIN' TO A BRAND NEW SOUND
HEY MAMA HEY MAMA, FOLLOW ME
I KNOW SOMETHING'S IN YOU THAT YOU WANNA SET FREE

SO LET GO, GO, GO OF THE PAST NOW
SAY HELLO TO THE LOVE IN YOUR HEART
YES, I KNOW THAT THE WORLD'S SPINNING FAST NOW
YOU GOTTA GET YOURSELF A BRAND NEW START

We also considered a bookie, a civil engineer, a contractor, and a parole officer.

Thank you, Harvey Fierstein!

This replaced the poetic but less funny "I haven't been out on the town since your baptism breakfast!"

Relatively new in the '60s: space travel, LSD, the topless bathing suit, seatbelts, Liberty and Equality for All.

This was the second song written for the score. "Welcome to the '60s" is a line in the original movie, spoken by Ricki Lake as TRACY TURNBLAD.

DYNAMITES	BACKUP
HEY MAMA	
WELCOME TO THE SIXTIES	WELCOME TO THE SIXTIES!
OH-O-O-O-O	
OH MAMA	
WELCOME TO THE SIXTIES	WELCOME TO THE SIXTIES!
OH-O-O-O-O	
OH MAMA	
GO, GO, GO!	GO, GO, GO!
	WELCOME TO THE SIXTIES
	WO OO OO OO OO OH
	HEY-A MAMA
	YEAH, YEAH, YEAH,
	YEAH, YEAH, YEAH

(TRACY and EDNA hit the streets of Baltimore for
a fashion and hair makeover.)

TRACY
HEY MAMA, HEY MAMA,
TAKE MY HAND

EDNA
FIRST LET'S MAKE A PIT STOP AT
THE WIENER STAND

TRACY
HEY MAMA, HEY MAMA,
TAKE A CHANCE

EDNA
TRACY, IT'S BEEN YEARS
SINCE SOMEONE ASKED ME TO DANCE

TRACY & DYNAMITES
SO LET GO, GO, GO

TRACY
OF THE PAST NOW

TRACY & DYNAMITES
SAY HELLO

TRACY
TO THE LIGHT IN YOUR EYES
YES, I KNOW THAT THE WORLD'S SPINNING FAST NOW
YA GOTTA RUN THE RACE TO WIN THE PRIZE

DYNAMITES
HOO HOO HOO
OOH OOH OOH

ALL
HEY MAMA, WELCOME TO THE SIXTIES
OH OH OH OH OH OH OH OH
OH MAMA, WELCOME TO THE SIXTIES
OH OH OH OH OH OH OH
GO MAMA, GO, GO, GO!

WELCOME TO THE SIXTIES
OH OH OH OH OH
HEY, MAMA
YEAH, YEAH, YEAH
YEAH, YEAH, YEAH

(They arrive at THE HEFTY HIDEAWAY to find
MR. PINKY giving away free doughnuts.)

MR. PINKY
Free jelly doughnuts while they last. Eat 'em up,
girls. I've got ten tons of taffeta inside.

TRACY
Hello, Mr. Pinky. I'm Tracy.

MR. PINKY
There's my shining star! Television doesn't do
you justice.

The thrill this trio gives the audience is one of the show's happiest moments. The DYNAMITES stepping right out of their poster is a great idea of Jerry Mitchell's.

COMEDY THEORY: Alliteration leads to laffs!

There's a similar joke in The Producers, but that's what EDNA is—a Mother Load!

Some inspiration for the Dynamites

EDNA

Oh, Mr. Pinky, you certainly picked a lovely girl to put the plus in your plus-sizes.

MR. PINKY

Now, Tracy, this can't be your agent. She must be your gorgeous, big sister.

EDNA

(squealing with delight)
Why, Mr. Pinky, you're twisting my head! I'm not her gorgeous, big sister, I'm . . .

MR. PINKY

. . . 54 Double D?

EDNA

Triple E!!!

MR. PINKY

Oh, Mama, I've hit the motherlode! Step inside and let's make a deal.
(MR. PINKY and EDNA disappear into the store.)

ALL
YOUR MAMA'S WELCOMING THE SIXTIES
OH OH OH OH OH OH OH OH
YOUR MAMA'S WELCOMING THE SIXTIES
OH OH OH OH OH OH OH
GO MAMA, GO, GO, GO!
(FANS besiege TRACY for photos and autographs.)

DYNAMITES
WELCOME TO THE RHYTHM OF A BRAND NEW DAY

TRACY
TAKE YOUR OLD-FASHIONED FEARS

DYNAMITES
AND JUST THROW THEM AWAY

MR. PINKY'S STAFF
YOU SHOULD ADD SOME COLOR AND A FRESH NEW "DO"

DYNAMITES & ENSEMBLE
'CAUSE IT'S TIME FOR A STAR
WHO LOOKS JUST LIKE YOU!

Jack and Jerry urged us to write more for the DYNAMITES. These lyrics were written during Seattle previews to showcase these brilliant singers and give Harvey more time to change.

JUDINE
DON'TCHA LET NOBODY TRY TO STEAL YOUR FUN
'CAUSE A LITTLE TOUCH OF LIPSTICK NEVER HURT NO ONE

KAMILAH
THE FUTURE'S GOT A MILLION ROADS FOR YOU TO CHOOSE
BUT YOU'LL WALK A LITTLE TALLER IN SOME HIGH-HEEL SHOES

SHAYNA
AND ONCE YOU FIND THE STYLE
THAT MAKES YOU FEEL LIKE YOU
SOMETHING FRESH AND NEW

DYNAMITES
STEP ON OUT
HEAR US SHOUT

TRACY & DYNAMITES
MAMA, THAT'S YOUR CUE!!!
YEAH, YEAH, YEAH

(EDNA emerges from the shop looking resplendent.)

EDNA
HEY TRACY, HEY TRACY,
LOOK AT ME!
I'M THE CUTEST CHICKIE
THAT YA EVER DID SEE

HEY TRACY, HEY BABY,
LOOK AT US
WHERE IS THERE A TEAM
THAT'S HALF AS FABULOUS?!

My Fair Lady meets a pit stop at the Indianapolis 500.

(TRACY enters THE HEFTY HIDEAWAY.)

ALL
I LET GO, GO, GO

EDNA
OF THE PAST NOW

ALL
SAID HELLO

EDNA
TO THIS RED CARPET RIDE

Act One Scene 7

I had this new idea for a variation of EDNA's verse. . . . I said, "Scott, what's a five-syllable (with a pushed third syllable) name of a sex symbol of the day who EDNA can fantasize being like?" Scott sucked up a cigarette and said "Lollabrigida."

ALL
YES, I KNOW

EDNA
THAT THE WORLD'S SPINNING FAST NOW
TELL LOLLABRIGIDA TO STEP ASIDE!

EDNA
YOUR MAMA'S
WELCOMING THE SIXTIES
OH-O-O-O-O

OH MAMA'S
WELCOMING THE SIXTIES
OH-O-O-O-O

ALL
OPEN THE DOOR FOR THE GIRL
WHO HAS MORE, SHE'S A STAR
TRACY, GO, GO, GO!
(TRACY reenters in a matching outfit.)

TRACY & EDNA	BACKUP
HEY MAMA	
WELCOME TO THE SIXTIES	WELCOME TO THE SIXTIES
OH-O-O-O-O	
OH MAMA	WO, OH, OH, OH
WELCOME TO THE SIXTIES	WELCOME TO THE SIXTIES
OH-O-O-O-O	OH, OH, OH, OH
GO MAMA	WO, OH, OH, OH
GO, GO, GO!	GO, GO, GO!
WELCOME TO THE SIXTIES	WELCOME TO THE SIXTIES
	GO MAMA
	OH, OH, OH, OH
	WO, OH, OH, OH
GO MAMA	GO MAMA
GO, GO, GO!	GO, GO, GO!

Inspiration for the set of the Hefty Hideaway!

The Bible says something about "The glamour of the mother is revisited upon the daughter."

Designing *Hairspray*

David Rockwell, Set Designer

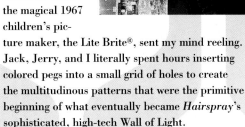

Strange as it may seem, in 1968, when I was ten years old, my family moved from the New Jersey shore to Guadalajara, Mexico. For the next eight years, my version of popular culture revolved around Cantinflas and bullfights. When I returned to the United States to study architecture at Syracuse University, I quickly discovered that the American popular culture that my fellow students took for granted was so new to me that it filled me with wonder and surprise.

That point of view proved to be great preparation when I set out to create the world of *Hairspray*.

Three principles guided me while I worked on the show. Set in 1962, *Hairspray* is told through the eyes of chubby, teenage freedom-fighter/dancing queen Tracy Turnblad. The first thing I had to do was find the visual vocabulary for the wonder and surprise that characterize Tracy's optimistic point of view. As written, the show breezes through eighteen different locations with almost no time for transitions. Next, I had to create visual transitions from one scene to another that occurred so quickly they would never interfere with what director Jack O'Brien and choreographer Jerry Mitchell called the "locomotive" of the show. Finally, I had to create three different realities: the world of white Baltimore, that of African-American Baltimore, and the integrated world that *Hairspray* celebrates.

Not too long after I signed on to the project, Jack proposed a trip to Baltimore so that he, Jerry, and I could see Tracy's hometown with our own eyes. The pilgrimage took on a magical glow that would pervade the entire *Hairspray* experience when Baltimore's favorite son, John Waters, volunteered to be our tour guide.

The city that John placed on display that day—much of it unchanged over the past forty years—amazed me. I was intrigued to discover that, until the 1950s, the row house was Baltimore's primary housing form and that an individual color scheme was the sole design element that proudly differentiated one dwelling from another.

To add to my fascination, a faux-stone exterior siding known as Formstone™ fronted many houses. My job would be to capture the distinctive spirit of the city without placing undue emphasis on gritty urban reality.

John, who is one of our great comic filmmakers, views his birthplace with heartfelt affection (so much so that in 1985, the city fathers established an annual John Waters Day). That fondness is amplified by a baroque style that seems to suggest that Vincente Minnelli has run wild in the most unlikely urban setting imaginable. Filmed in 1988, John's film *Hairspray* filtered the Baltimore of his 1960s adolescence through his then-contemporary 1980s experience. It fell to me to devise twenty-first century theatrical equivalents for John's iconoclastic approach.

Accomplishing those goals involved an enormous amount of visual archaeology, and my associate designers, Richard Jaris and Barry Richards, and I spent three feverish months collecting and poring over what seemed to be literally tons of visual material. As photographs flowed into my office, they were sorted by category ("HAIR," "MUSIC," "FURNITURE") and then mounted on seventeen large boards. The search for images that would stimulate the theatrical imagination also involved a rigorous inspection of toys, products, and tapes of television shows of the period.

As with any creative experience, there are breakthrough moments. The one I will remember most occurred when the magical 1967 children's picture maker, the Lite Brite®, sent my mind reeling. Jack, Jerry, and I literally spent hours inserting colored pegs into a small grid of holes to create the multitudinous patterns that were the primitive beginning of what eventually became *Hairspray*'s sophisticated, high-tech Wall of Light.

It amazed and thrilled me (but should not have surprised me) when all the elements of the show came together seamlessly. Theater is the most collaborative art form, bringing together individuals with diverse skills who contribute their talents to achieve a common goal. The heart of *Hairspray*—both the movie and the musical—encompasses John Waters's belief in racial, sexual, class, and body-type tolerance. Although it went unspoken, as a result of September 11, 2001, every member of the *Hairspray* family realized the significance of transferring John's vision of empowerment and hopefulness to the stage. Trust, respect, and flexibility underpinned the desire to accomplish our shared goal. Belonging to this creative, dedicated, and loving group of theatrical artists reinforced my passion for the theater and my desire to continue working in it.

SHOW CURTAIN: The first thing I wanted the audience to see was a giant-size representation of the biggest bouffant in Broadway history, seemingly made of real hair. The idea of creating this towering hairdo went through a number of permutations. During the "Hairspray" production number, our final version, a show curtain consisting of seven miles of quarter-inch rubber tubing lifts and frames the stage in the emblematic shape of a flip hairdo.

COLOR SCHEME: The appealing, pastel-colored palette of Necco® Wafers inspired the color scheme of some of the sets.

"GOOD MORNING BALTIMORE": The streetscape features our theatricalized, painted version of the Formstone™ look. The second time the audience sees the row houses their window screens have been decorated with hand-painted retro patterns based on space-age fabric design. This authentic visual touch is meant to suggest that Baltimore has entered the 1960s.

The latticework of booms and microphones on *The Corny Collins Show* commemorates Boris Aronson's set designs for the musical *Do-Re-Mi*. The gold-toned false proscenium suggests the shape of a 1960s television set.

TOYS WERE—AND ARE—US: Could a large number of LED light sources be programmed to create an animated wall of light reflective of the style of the Lite Brite®? We wondered. And could that wall subsequently add an effective landscape of color and pattern to the show? In order to find the answers, we first produced a series of animated videos. When they clearly demonstrated that mating 1960s nostalgia to state-of-the-art technology would add a whole new visual landscape to the show, we knew our creation was here to stay. Along with circles and ovals, the dots in the Lite Brite® represent one of the most frequently occurring motifs in 1960s design. Even the balloons that hang in the Patterson Park High School gymnasium contain dots in their design.

93

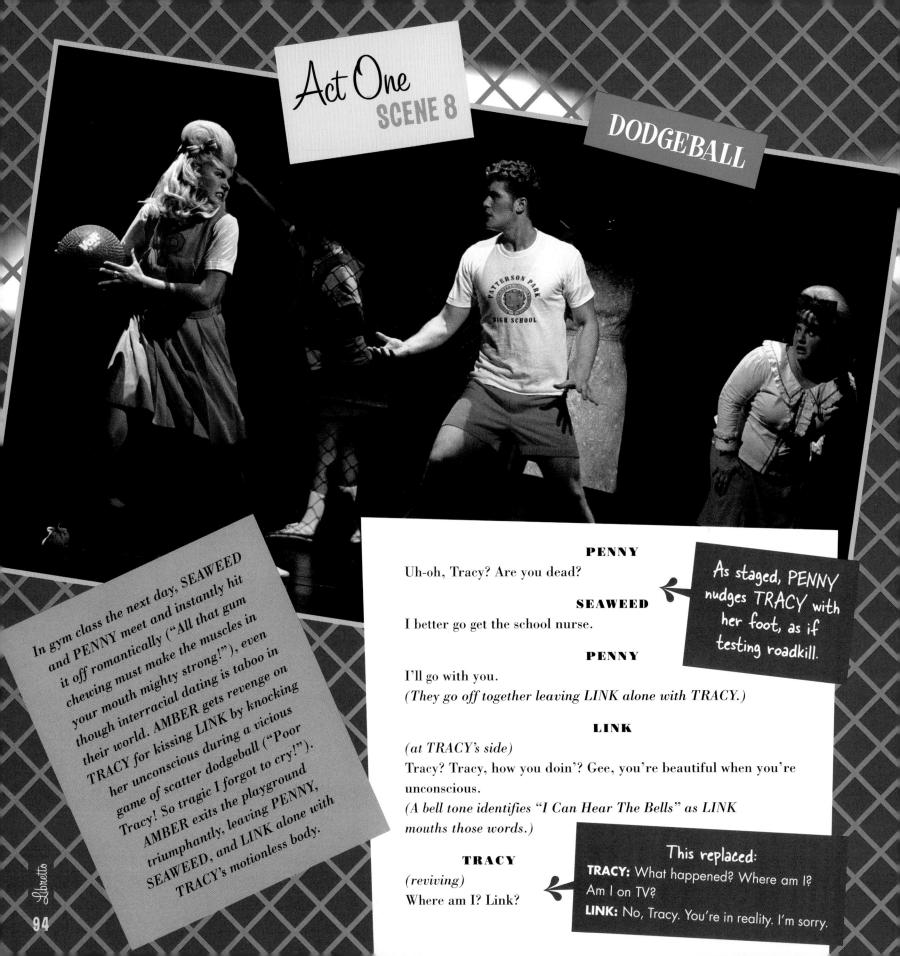

DODGEBALL

In gym class the next day, SEAWEED and PENNY meet and instantly hit it off romantically ("All that gum chewing must make the muscles in your mouth mighty strong!"), even though interracial dating is taboo in their world. AMBER gets revenge on TRACY for kissing LINK by knocking her unconscious during a vicious game of scatter dodgeball ("Poor Tracy! So tragic I forgot to cry!"). AMBER exits the playground triumphantly, leaving PENNY, SEAWEED, and LINK alone with TRACY's motionless body.

PENNY

Uh-oh, Tracy? Are you dead?

SEAWEED

I better go get the school nurse.

PENNY

I'll go with you.
(They go off together leaving LINK alone with TRACY.)

LINK

(at TRACY's side)
Tracy? Tracy, how you doin'? Gee, you're beautiful when you're unconscious.
(A bell tone identifies "I Can Hear The Bells" as LINK mouths those words.)

TRACY

(reviving)
Where am I? Link?

As staged, PENNY nudges TRACY with her foot, as if testing roadkill.

This replaced:
TRACY: What happened? Where am I? Am I on TV?
LINK: No, Tracy. You're in reality. I'm sorry.

LINK

You better? For a second there it looked like "Teen Angel" time.

TRACY

(into LINK's eyes)
Wherever I am, please, no one change the channel.

LINK

You've got a funny way of putting things. I like that.

PENNY

(returning with SEAWEED)
The nurse is out sick, but look what Seaweed found.

SEAWEED

(removing the stuff from his pocket)
Band-Aids and Q-Tips! Oh, and a rubber. No, I guess that's mine.

PENNY

He's so nurturing.

TRACY

Oh, Link, this is my friend Seaweed.
(The BOYS grunt toward each other.)

LINK

How you doin'?

SEAWEED

How you doin'?

PENNY

(to TRACY)
How are you doing?

TRACY

How do you think? I just got creamed in front of the entire school.

SEAWEED

Hey, Trace, I know what'll make you feel better. My mom's pitchin' a platter party at our record shop on North Avenue. Wanna come check it out?

PENNY

I, too, feel not good. May I also come check it out?

SEAWEED

You surely may.

cf. "Physician, heal thyself"!

"Rubber" is slang for a condom. Boys in the '60s carried them but never got a chance to use them.

Uneasy, but not hostile.

Alternately, "mertilized."

Response cut after charges of corniness: "No, I Penny Lou!"

TRACY

I've never been to North Avenue before.

LINK

Would it be safe up there for, you know, us?

SEAWEED

Don't worry, cracker boy, it's cool.

TRACY

What do you think, Link?

LINK

I think getting to know you is the beginning of a whole lot of adventure.

PENNY

Imagine being invited places by colored people.

TRACY

It feels so hip!

SEAWEED

Glad you feel that way, friends. 'Cause not everybody does.

"RUN AND TELL THAT!"

Here comes that Motown sound!

SEAWEED
I CAN'T SEE
WHY PEOPLE LOOK AT ME
AND ONLY SEE
THE COLOR OF MY FACE

AND THEN THERE'S THOSE
THAT TRY TO HELP, GOD KNOWS
BUT ALWAYS HAVE TO
PUT ME IN MY PLACE

NOW I WON'T ASK YOU
TO BE COLOR BLIND
'CAUSE IF YOU PICK THE FRUIT
THEN, GIRL, YOU'RE SURE TO FIND

THE BLACKER THE BERRY
THE SWEETER THE JUICE
I COULD SAY IT AIN'T SO
BUT, DARLIN', WHAT'S THE USE

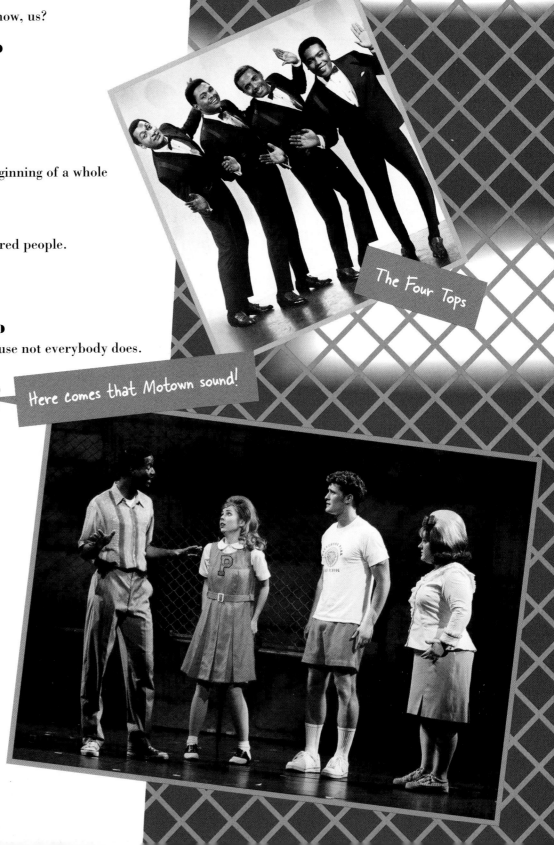

The Four Tops

SEAWEED (cont'd)	BACKUP (cont'd)
THE DARKER THE CHOCOLATE	
THE RICHER THE TASTE	
AND THAT'S WHERE IT'S AT . . .	
. . . NOW RUN AND TELL THAT!!	
	RUN AND TELL THAT!
RUN AND TELL THAT!	
	RUN AND TELL THAT!
I CAN'T SEE	I CAN'T SEE
WHY PEOPLE DISAGREE	OOH'S
EACH TIME I TELL THEM	
WHAT I KNOW IS TRUE	
AND IF YOU COME	AND IF YOU COME
AND SEE THE WORLD I'M FROM	OOH'S
I BET YOUR HEART	
IS GONNA FEEL IT TOO	
YEAH, I COULD LIE	
BUT, BABY, LET'S BE BOLD	
VANILLA CAN BE NICE	VANILLA CAN BE NICE
BUT IF THE TRUTH BE TOLD	UH-HUH
THE BLACKER THE BERRY	OO
THE SWEETER THE JUICE	UH-HUH
I COULD SAY IT AIN'T SO	
BUT, DARLIN', WHAT'S THE USE	OO-OO
THE DARKER THE CHOCOLATE	OO
THE RICHER THE TASTE	
AND THAT'S WHERE IT'S AT . . .	AND THAT'S WHERE IT'S AT - WOO!
. . . NOW RUN AND TELL THAT!!	
	RUN AND TELL THAT!
RUN AND TELL THAT	
	RUN AND TELL THAT!
RUN AND TELL THAT	
	RUN AND TELL THAT!
RUN AND TELL THAT	
	RUN AND TELL THAT!

(The song continues as we segue directly into . . .)

The expression "run and tell that" comes from a brilliant dictionary called Black Talk. A good book to read on the subway.

THE RECORD SHOP

Act One
SCENE 9

(MOTORMOUTH MAYBELLE's record shop. LITTLE INEZ and other BLACK TEENS are dancing as SEAWEED, PENNY, TRACY, and LINK arrive. MUSIC continues under the dialogue.)

LITTLE INEZ

Hey, you're Tracy. You're my favorite dancer on *The Corny Collins Show*.

SEAWEED

This is my sister, Little Inez.

TRACY

Sure. I saw you at the auditions.

LITTLE INEZ

Well, you're the only one who did, 'cause they kicked me out on my young, gifted, and black behind.

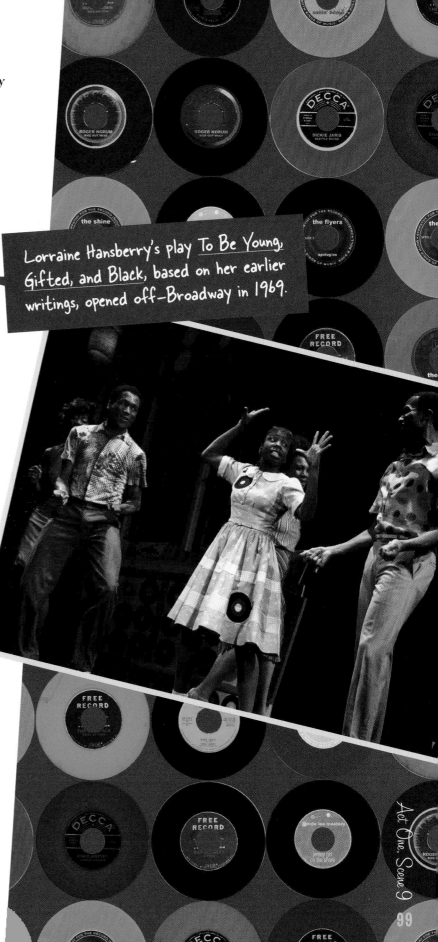

Lorraine Hansberry's play To Be Young, Gifted, and Black, based on her earlier writings, opened off-Broadway in 1969.

LITTLE INEZ	BACKUP
I'M TIRED OF COVERIN' UP	(HAND CLAPS)
ALL MY PRIDE	
SO GIVE ME FIVE	SO GIVE ME FIVE
ON THE BLACK-HAND SIDE	ON THE BLACK-HAND SIDE
I'VE GOT A NEW WAY OF MOVIN'	
AND I GOT MY OWN VOICE	
SO HOW CAN I HELP	SO HOW CAN I HELP
BUT TO SHOUT AND REJOICE	BUT TO SHOUT AND REJOICE
PEOPLE 'ROUND HERE	OOH . . .
CAN BARELY PAY THEIR RENT	
THEY'RE "TRY'N TO MAKE DOLLAR	OOH . . .
OUTA FIFTEEN CENT"	
BUT WE GOT A SPIRIT	OOH . . .
MONEY JUST CAN'T BUY	
IT'S DEEP AS A RIVER	IT'S DEEP AS A RIVER
AND SOARS TO THE SKY!!	AND SOARS TO THE SKY!!

SEAWEED

I CAN'T SEE	I CAN'T SEE
THE REASON IT CAN'T BE	
THE KINDA WORLD	
WHERE WE ALL GET OUR CHANCE	(AD LIBS)
THE TIME IS NOW	THE TIME IS NOW
AND WE CAN SHOW 'EM HOW	
JUST TURN THE MUSIC UP	
AND LET'S ALL DANCE	

SEAWEED	BACKUP
'CAUSE ALL THINGS ARE EQUAL	OOH'S
WHEN IT COMES TO LOVE	
WELL, THAT'S NOT QUITE TRUE	
'CAUSE WHEN PUSH COMES TO SHOVE . . .	HUH
THE BLACKER THE BERRY	OO
THE SWEETER THE JUICE	UH-HUH
I COULD SAY IT AIN'T SO	
BUT, DARLIN', WHAT'S THE USE	OO-OO
THE DARKER THE CHOCOLATE	OO
THE RICHER THE TASTE	
AND THAT'S WHERE IT'S AT . . .	AND THAT'S WHERE IT'S AT - WOO
. . . NOW RUN AND TELL THAT!!	
	RUN AND TELL THAT
RUN AND TELL THAT	
	RUN AND TELL THAT
YOU BETTER RUN AND TELL THAT	
	RUN AND TELL THAT
RUN AND TELL THAT	

(The song ends and MOTORMOUTH makes her entrance.)

DRAMATIC THEORY: It can add excitement and a new burst of energy to meet one of the principal players late in the show.

Libretto

MOTORMOUTH

There's platters of tunes and food on the table.
What else would you expect from . . .

ALL

Miz Motormouth Maybelle!

SEAWEED

Mama, I brought some friends.

MOTORMOUTH

Whoop-dee-doo, what a coup! The ever
sparkin' Sir Link Larkin!

LINK

Always nice to see you, Miz Motormouth.

PENNY

I'm Penny Lou Pingleton and I'm very pleased
and scared to be here.

MOTORMOUTH

You're welcome, Kitten, to come and sit in.

TRACY

This is just so Afro-tastic. Can I say how thrilled I am
to meet you, Miz Motormouth. I'm Seaweed's friend, Tracy.

MOTORMOUTH

Oh, yes, indeedy. I've seen you, sweetie. All aglow on
Corny's show.

TRACY

Gee, thanks. But I'm only there because of your son. Why can't
we all dance together like this on TV?

MOTORMOUTH

Think we haven't tried? We've pleaded, begged,
and lied. We pressured the Mayor, petitioned the
Gov, and what did we get?

MOTORMOUTH & KIDS

One day a month.

SEAWEED

Enough talk. We came to dance. Let's play
some hide and seek!
(*MUSIC starts.*)

ANACHRONISM WATCH: It's a bit early to use "Afro," but it was too much fun not to.

The 1964 Civil Rights Act is not far off.

CUT

PENNY: They can't do that! It's unethnical!

Act One, Scene 9

103

John Waters favored a dirty boogie called the Bodie Green.

TRACY, PENNY, & LINK

The Dirty Boogie!
(They start to dance when the door suddenly bursts open.)

AMBER

Aaaaaaiiiiiieeeeeee!!!! Link! What are you doing in this huge crowd of minorities?

LINK

Trying to fit in. What are you doing?

COMEDY THEORY: Villains always reveal their idiocy by accident.

AMBER

I waited for you under the bleachers halfway through the JV track meet, then I saw you getting on the North Avenue bus and I followed you here in my new car.

LINK

We're having a blast. Come, jump in.
(The door bursts open again.)

It's a Corvette, in our minds.

VELMA

Aaaaaaaaiiiiiiieeeeeee!!!!! Amber! Has anyone touched you?

MOTORMOUTH

Y'all better hustle. Here's Von Tussle.

VELMA

I saw you getting into your darling new car, so I followed you in mine. Motormouth, are you brainwashing these children?

MOTORMOUTH

They're only dancing.

An Oldsmobile, we imagine.

TRACY

Yeah, we're dancing.

VELMA

(taking in TRACY)
Oh! I should have known you'd be at the bottom of this barrel.
(The door opens again and this time EDNA enters with a take-out bag.)

COMEDY THEORY: Three times is the charm.

EDNA

Oooooooooohhhhhh!!!!!! Tracy, that was you I saw!
(calling out the door)
Wilbur! It was the kids I saw.

Libretto

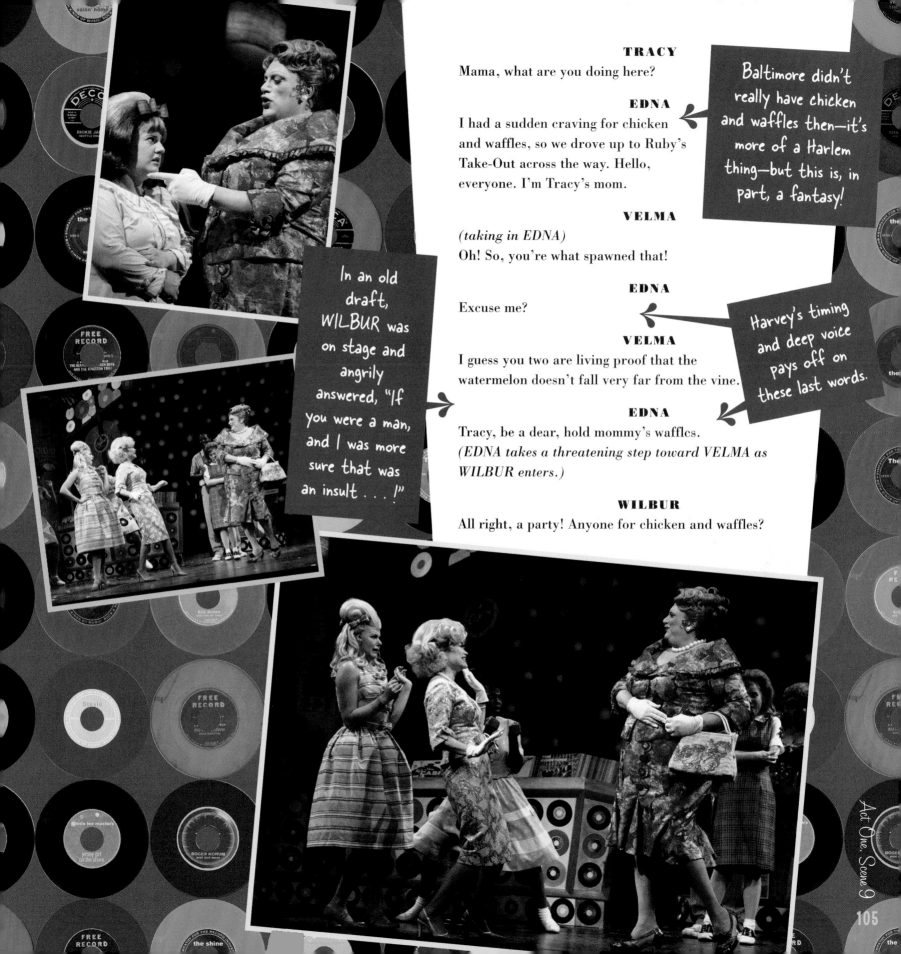

TRACY

Mama, what are you doing here?

EDNA

I had a sudden craving for chicken and waffles, so we drove up to Ruby's Take-Out across the way. Hello, everyone. I'm Tracy's mom.

VELMA

(taking in EDNA)
Oh! So, you're what spawned that!

EDNA

Excuse me?

VELMA

I guess you two are living proof that the watermelon doesn't fall very far from the vine.

EDNA

Tracy, be a dear, hold mommy's waffles.
(EDNA takes a threatening step toward VELMA as WILBUR enters.)

WILBUR

All right, a party! Anyone for chicken and waffles?

Baltimore didn't really have chicken and waffles then—it's more of a Harlem thing—but this is, in part, a fantasy!

In an old draft, WILBUR was on stage and angrily answered, "If you were a man, and I was more sure that was an insult . . . !"

Harvey's timing and deep voice pays off on these last words.

CINDY WATKINS

If we get any more white people in here, it'll be a suburb.

> This was the last new line added to the show, a week before we opened.

> "Suburb" is a very post-World War II word.

VELMA

(starting toward the door)
Come on, Amber. Let's get back to the right side of the tracks, if our cars are still there.

AMBER

(following VELMA)
Let's go, Link.

> In the movie, PRUDY appears in the record shop, but not VELMA, AMBER, EDNA, or WILBUR.

LINK

Amber, you're being rude to these people.

VELMA

(as if to a dog)
Amber. Come!

AMBER

(just like Mama)
Link. Come!
(He doesn't move.)
Link! Come!!!

LINK

Amber. Go.

AMBER

(trying to save face)
What ever happened to the bland, spineless boy I fell in love with? Mother, come.
(She marches out the door.)

> See? LINK's growing already.

VELMA

With pleasure.
(They are gone. A pause and then . . .)

EDNA

I didn't care for them.

> COMEDY THEORY: Flat understatement.

LITTLE INEZ

Are all white people like that?

WILBUR

Naw. . . . Just most.

Libretto

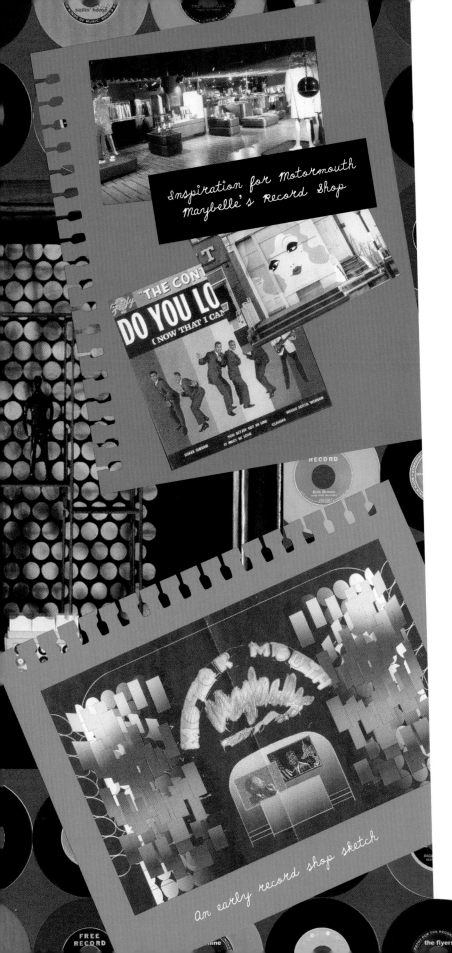

Inspiration for Motormouth Maybelle's Record Shop

an early record shop sketch

TRACY

Well, I know how we can start changing that. If kids saw us dancing together on TV they'd realize that we're not so different after all. We just want to have a good time.

SEAWEED

You saying you and Link would be willing to dance with us on Negro Day? That would be earthshaking!

LINK

(getting nervous)
Tracy . . .

TRACY

No. We're not going to dance on Negro Day.

LINK

(relieved)
Whew.

PARALLEL SITUATION: Would Pat Boone march to ban the bomb?

TRACY

(pointing to MOTORMOUTH)
You're going to crash White Day!

MOTORMOUTH

White Day is every day. Ya gotta get more specific than that!

TRACY

Is tomorrow specific enough? Think: It's Mother-Daughter Day. Miz Motormouth, you work for the station. They could never turn you and Little Inez away. And once the two of you break the barrier, we'll all be free to dance on TV.

SEAWEED

That thinking's downright revolutionary.

LITTLE INEZ

We'll set off sparks, like Rosa Parks!

cf. Langston Hughes: "I love you, Ralph Bunche, but I can't eat you for lunch!"

(But LINK is too anxious about becoming a big star to risk any controversy. He leaves, breaking TRACY's heart. Still, wise, tender EDNA comforts her, and they all resolve to go ahead with the Mother-Daughter Day protest. EDNA just needs a little coaching to overcome her camera shyness.)

Act One, Scene 9

EDNA

I'm sorry, Tracy. But no one said anything about me appearing on television. I'm sorry but I simply cannot appear on television at my present weight.

MOTORMOUTH

You can't let weight restrict your fate! Look at me! I'm on TV!

EDNA

Oh, but Miz Motormouth, you're a celebrity. While I'm a simple housewife of indeterminate girth.

MOTORMOUTH

The bigger the girth, the more you're worth! Mr. Turnblad, you don't mind that the missus here is an ample American, do you?

WILBUR

Not at all. I think of her as prime real estate.

MOTORMOUTH

Yeah! Nice and roomy. You listen to me!

"BIG, BLONDE AND BEAUTIFUL"

MOTORMOUTH
ONCE UPON A TIME
GIRL, I WAS JUST LIKE YOU
NEVER LET MY EXTRA LARGE
LARGESSE SHINE THROUGH

HAIR WAS BROWN AND NAPPY
NEVER HAD NO FUN
I HID UNDER A BUSHEL
WHICH IS EASIER SAID THAN DONE!

THEN ONE DAY MY GRANDMA
WHO WAS BIG AND STOUT
SHE SAID YOU GOTTA LOVE YOURSELF
FROM INSIDE OUT

WILBUR: But we'll sign any petition you want! Twice!

ANACHRONISM WATCH: Afro-American was not quite common parlance in 1962, but Irish American and Italian American, etc., were.

MOTORMOUTH (cont'd)
AND JUST AS SOON AS I LEARNED
HOW TO STRUT MY FUNKY STUFF
I FOUND OUT THAT
THE WORLD AT LARGE
CAN'T GET ENOUGH SO

BRING ON THAT PECAN PIE
POUR SOME SUGAR ON IT,
SUGAR, DON'T BE SHY

SCOOP ME UP A MESS
OF THAT CHOCOLATE SWIRL
DON'T BE STINGY,
I'M A GROWING GIRL

"BIG, BLONDE AND BEAUTIFUL"
This was one of the first songs written.
    Since we wrote this song as a sort of "stand-alone" number for MOTORMOUTH, over the course of rehearsals we rewrote large portions of it to help tie the song more into what is happening in the plot. The intro, for instance: We wrote it while walking to the Empire Diner in Manhattan. Once again, food and Hairspray coincide.
    We also knew that either this song or "Welcome to the '60s" should end Act I, but no one could come up with how to do it until Jack and Jerry came along. They suggested, "Cut the scene and song that comprise the protest rally and make it all part of this song." Such talented boys. (The cut song was the mother-daughter cha-cha-cha below.)

AMBER
SHE'S ALWAYS THERE TO HELP ME
WITH MY HOMEWORK AND MY HAIR
SHE'S ALWAYS THERE ADVISING ME
ON WHAT TO THINK AND WEAR

VELMA
AND EVEN ON YOUR HONEYMOON
LOOK UP AND I'LL BE THERE

BOTH
THAT'S THE MOTHER-DAUGHTER CHA-CHA-CHA

VELMA
I ALWAYS HAVE TO FIGHT OFF
ALL HER TEENAGE ROMEOS
THANK GOD I KEPT MY FIGURE
I CAN BORROW ALL HER CLOTHES

AMBER
WE'LL REALLY LOOK LIKE TWINS
THE DAY YOU BUY ME MY NEW NOSE

BOTH
THAT'S THE MOTHER-DAUGHTER CHA-CHA-CHA

AMBER
SHE HAS A LIST OF DATING DOS AND DON'TS
A MILE LONG

VELMA
LIKE LET THEM THINK YOU MIGHT
BUT KEEP THOSE KNEECAPS TIGHT!

AMBER
SHE BUYS ME LOTS OF MAKEUP

VELMA
(EVEN GOD GETS SOME THINGS WRONG)

AMBER
BUT MUST YOU SQUEEZE EACH PORE

VELMA
THAT'S WHAT A MOTHER'S FOR!

AMBER
AND SO LADIES AND GENTLEMEN
I'M SURE YOU'D ALL AGREE
"MISS HAIRSPRAY" IS MY BIRTHRIGHT
OH, AND THIS I GUARANTEE

VELMA
IF YOU DON'T VOTE FOR HER
WELL THEN YOU'LL HAVE TO DEAL WITH ME

BOTH
THAT'S THE MOTHER DAUGHTER
THAT'S THE MOTHER DAUGHTER
THAT'S THE MOTHER DAUGHTER CHA CHA
CHA

AMBER
SHE PUTS ME ON A DIET
EVERY TIME I HAVE A DATE

VELMA
A TEENAGE GIRL MUST MAKE A FRIEND WITH
HUNGER

AMBER
SHE SAYS THAT TIME'S A-WASTING
AND I BETTER FIND MATE

VELMA
YOU'RE SIXTEEN . . . YOU AIN'T GETTING ANY
YOUNGER!

AMBER
SHE'S MY MOTHER AND MY BEST FRIEND
SPEC'LY ON A SHOPPING SPREE
BUT WHEN THE FUN IS OVER
AND THE GOOD LORD CALLS ON ME

VELMA
I'LL MEETCHA UP IN HEAVEN
WHERE WE'LL SPEND ETERNITY

BOTH
DOIN' THE MOTHER-DAUGHTER
YES THE MOTHER-DAUGHTER
THAT'S THE MOTHER-DAUGHTER CHA-CHA-CHA

MOTORMOUTH (cont'd)

I OFFER BIG LOVE
WITH NO APOLOGY
HOW CAN I DENY THE WORLD
THE MOST OF ME

I AM NOT AFRAID
TO THROW MY WEIGHT AROUND
POUND BY POUND BY POUND
BECAUSE I'M
BIG, BLONDE AND BEAUTIFUL
THERE IS NOTHIN' 'BOUT ME
THAT'S UNSUITABLE

NO ONE WANTS A MEAL
THAT ONLY OFFERS THE LEAST
WHEN, GIRL, WE'RE SERVING UP
THE WHOLE DAMN FEAST

MOTORMOUTH	**BACKUP**
	OOH OO OO, OOH OO OO!
SLICE OFF A PIECE	
OF THAT HOG HEAD CHEESE	
THEN TAKE A LOOK INSIDE	
MY BOOK OF RECIPES	
NOW, DON'T YOU SNIFF AROUND	*HOO - HOO - OOH - OOO*
FOR SOMETHING FLUFFY AND LIGHT	*. . . FLUFFY AND LIGHT*
I NEED A MAN	
WHO BRINGS A MAN-SIZE APPETITE	
I'LL USE A PINCH OF SUGAR	*. . . PINCH OF SUGAR*
AND A DASH OF SPICE	*AND A DASH OF SPICE*
I'LL LET YA LICK THE SPOON	
BECAUSE IT TASTES SO NICE	
I'LL KEEP IT IN MY OVEN	*HOO - HOO - OOH - OOO*
TILL IT'S GOOD AND HOT	*. . . GOOD AND HOT*
KEEP ON STIRRING	
TILL IT HITS THE SPOT	

Shades of "Jelly Roll" imagery in red hot mamas' repertory!

MOTORMOUTH (cont'd)
BECAUSE I'M
BIG, BLONDE AND BEAUTIFUL
AND EDNA, GIRL,
YOU'RE LOOKIN' SO RECRUITABLE
WHY SIT IN THE BLEACHERS
TIMID AND AFRAID
WHEN, EDNA,
YOU CAN BE YOUR OWN PARADE!

BACKUP (cont'd)

BIG, BLONDE AND BEAUTIFUL

HOO - OO - OO - OO - OO

COMEDY THEORY: The afterthought that admits the actual truth.

TRACY

So, how about it, Mama?

EDNA

Well, I am big, I am blonde . . . ish, and if you say I'm beautiful, I guess I'm beautiful. OK, I'll do it!
(*ALL cheer. The scene shifts and protest signs are distributed.*)

Act One, Scene 9

BACKUPS
OOH OO OO, OOH OO OO!

ALL
LOOK OUT
OLD BALTIMORE
WE'RE MARCHING IN
AND WE AIN'T SHUFFLIN'
THROUGH THAT OLD BACK DOOR

EDNA	**BACKUP**
AND TRACY, I WILL JOIN YOUR FIGHT	OOH-OOH-OOH
IF I CAN KEEP UP THIS PACE	

WILBUR
AND, GIRLS, I'LL BE RIGHT AT YOUR SIDE
IF I CAN FIND SOME SPACE

MOTORMOUTH	**BACKUP**
SO YOU CAN	HOOT!
HOLD YOUR HEAD UP	HOLD YOUR HEAD UP
JUST AS BIG AS YA PLEASE	JUST AS BIG AS YA PLEASE
YOU KNOW THEY'LL HEAR ME KNOCKIN'	
WITH THE TWO OF THESE!	OW!!

MOTORMOUTH, WILBUR, TRACY
TOMORROW, SIDE BY SIDE
WE'LL SHOW THE WORLD WHAT'S RIGHT

EDNA
LOOKS LIKE I'M TOUCHING UP MY ROOTS TONIGHT!

MOTORMOUTH	**BACKUP**
AND WE'LL BE	
BIG, BLONDE AND BEAUTIFUL	BIG, BLONDE AND BEAUTIFUL
SO FACE THE FACT	HOO-HOO
ITS SIMPLY IRREFUTABLE	HOO-HOO
CAN'T YA HEAR THAT RUMBLING?	HOO-00-00-00-00
THAT'S OUR HUNGER TO BE FREE	. . . HUNGER TO BE FREE
IT'S TIME TO FIN'LY TASTE EQUALITY	. . . FIN'LY TASTE EQUALITY

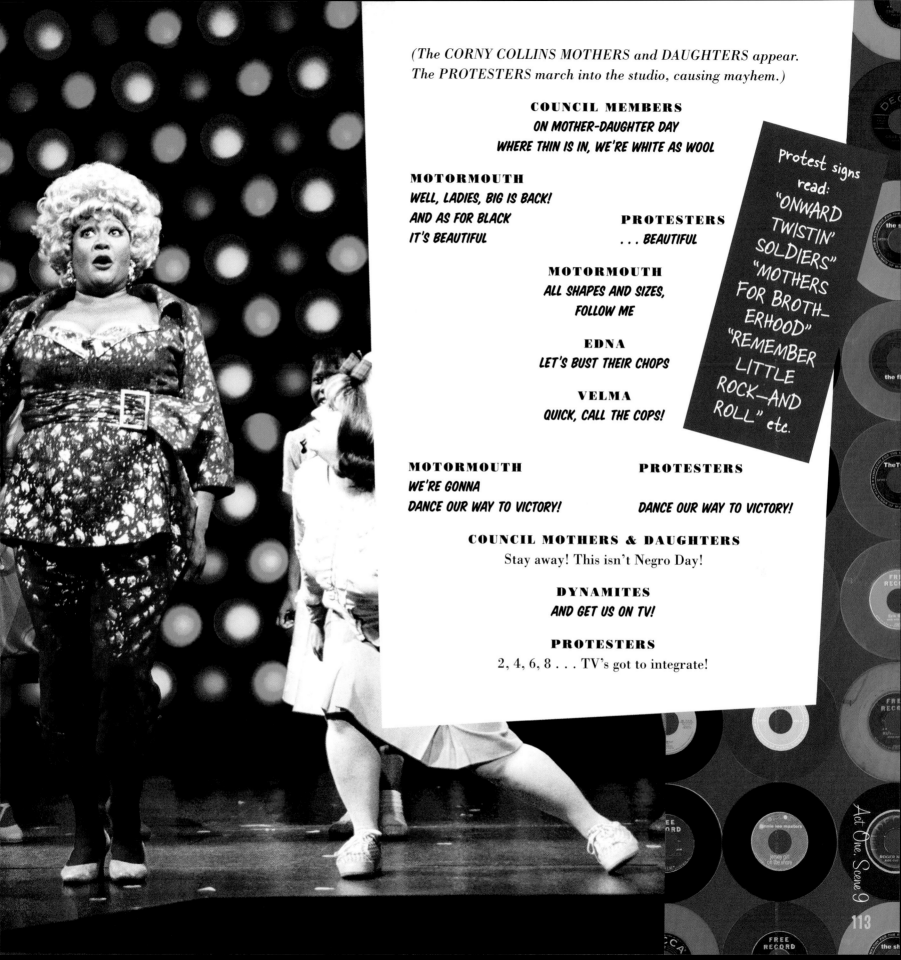

(The CORNY COLLINS MOTHERS and DAUGHTERS appear.
The PROTESTERS march into the studio, causing mayhem.)

COUNCIL MEMBERS
ON MOTHER-DAUGHTER DAY
WHERE THIN IS IN, WE'RE WHITE AS WOOL

MOTORMOUTH
WELL, LADIES, BIG IS BACK!
AND AS FOR BLACK   **PROTESTERS**
IT'S BEAUTIFUL   *. . . BEAUTIFUL*

MOTORMOUTH
ALL SHAPES AND SIZES,
FOLLOW ME

EDNA
LET'S BUST THEIR CHOPS

VELMA
QUICK, CALL THE COPS!

MOTORMOUTH   **PROTESTERS**
WE'RE GONNA
DANCE OUR WAY TO VICTORY!   *DANCE OUR WAY TO VICTORY!*

COUNCIL MOTHERS & DAUGHTERS
Stay away! This isn't Negro Day!

DYNAMITES
AND GET US ON TV!

PROTESTERS
2, 4, 6, 8 . . . TV's got to integrate!

protest signs read: "ONWARD TWISTIN' SOLDIERS" "MOTHERS FOR BROTHERHOOD" "REMEMBER LITTLE ROCK—AND ROLL" etc.

Act One, Scene 9

113

PROTESTERS

2, 4, 6, 8 . . . TV's got to integrate!

**COUNCIL MOTHERS
& DAUGHTERS**

Stay away! This isn't Negro Day!

DYNAMITES
AND GET US ON TV!

*(POLICE SIRENS wail. A PADDY WAGON backs in. Its doors open and
TWO OFFICERS emerge. As the PROTESTERS continue their march, they
are loaded into the PADDY WAGON.)*

MOTORMOUTH
We're here to dance!

EDNA
We're here to stay!

LINK
Tracy, this was beautiful!

MOTORMOUTH
BIG, BLONDE AND BEAUTIFUL LEAD THE WAY!

ALL
NO ONE'S GETTING ON TV TODAY!

(The CURTAIN falls on Act One.)

DRAMATIC THEORY: The Act
One curtain should fall on disaster,
active or impending.

Libretto

114

WOMEN'S HOUSE OF DETENTION

(The FEMALE CAST, with the exception of PRUDY, are in jail! A MATRON stands watch over them.)

WANTED

TRACY TURNBLAD

"BIG DOLLHOUSE"

WOMEN
I GOTTA GET OUT,
I GOTTA GET OUT,
I GOTTA GET OUT,
HOW'D I GET IN THIS SLAMMER
THIS COOLER,
THIS BIG DOLLHOUSE!

> Before the song was written, suggested titles included "Babes in Bondage," "Chicks in Chains," and "Heartache in Cellblock Six." We even considered "Female Trouble," a Waters film title.

MATRON
OK, ladies, welcome to the big dollhouse! For those of youse new to the penal system I'm letting you know now that I don't stand for boozing, doping, cussing, gambling, fighting, or any other sort of unladylike behavior. Think of me as a mother . . . who eats her young.

> Jackie Hoffman's joke.

VELMA
LOCKED UP WITH ALL THESE LOWLIFE WOMEN

EDNA
AND HORIZONTAL STRIPES
AIN'T EXACTLY SLIMMIN'

AMBER
IS THERE ANYBODY HERE WHO CAN DRYCLEAN MY BLOUSE?

MATRON
IT'S THE MAID'S DAY OFF

ALL
IN THE BIG DOLLHOUSE

LITTLE INEZ
LADY JUSTICE, WHERE HAVE YOU GONE?

EDNA
OOH, WILBUR, CHECK, I THINK I LEFT THE IRON ON!

VELMA
DID YOU SEE CORNY LAUGHING?
I COULD MURDER THAT LOUSE!

> He's the Democrat to her Republican.

ALL
HONEY, THAT'LL GETCHA LIFE
IN THE BIG DOLLHOUSE
BIG HOUSE!

VELMA
LOCKED UP HERE IN THE PEN

ALL
BIG HOUSE!

AMBER
NO PHONE!

EDNA
NO FOOD!

MOTORMOUTH
NO MEN!

EDNA
I NEED A CONJUGAL VISIT
FROM MY LOVING SPOUSE

MATRON
HONEY, JUST DROP THE SOAP

ALL
IN THE BIG DOLLHOUSE

MATRON
Exercise, ladies! Get in the trenches,
you wenches.

EDNA
YOO HOO, MY STOMACH'S A LITTLE SOUR
I HAVEN'T HAD FOOD
IN OVER AN HOUR

MATRON
YOU JUST HAD A PIZZA, MY KUGEL, A MOUSE!

ALL
THERE'S NO FOOD LEFT IN THE BIG DOLLHOUSE

VELMA
UH, MATRON,
I HAVE GOT TO COMPLAIN

HOOKER #2
MIRA, MAMI, DON'T I KNOW YOU
FROM FIRST AND MAIN?

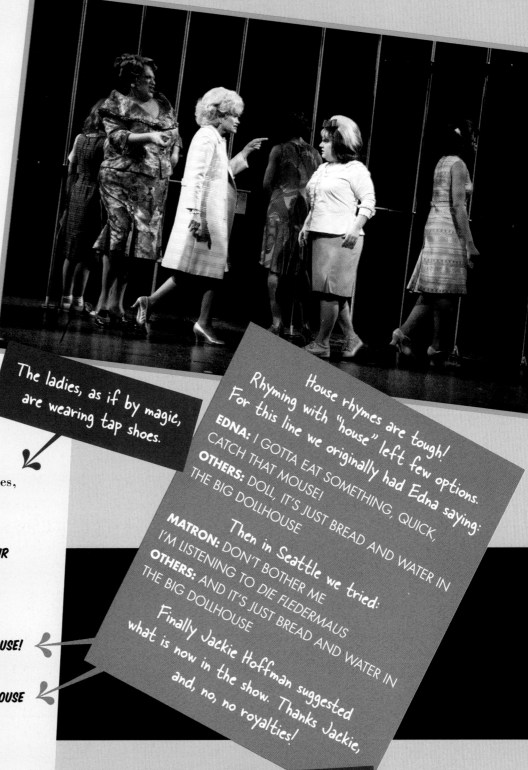

The ladies, as if by magic, are wearing tap shoes.

House rhymes are tough! Rhyming with "house" left few options. For this line we originally had Edna saying:
EDNA: I GOTTA EAT SOMETHING, QUICK, CATCH THAT MOUSE!
OTHERS: DOLL, IT'S JUST BREAD AND WATER IN THE BIG DOLLHOUSE

Then in Seattle we tried:
MATRON: DON'T BOTHER ME I'M LISTENING TO DIE FLEDERMAUS
OTHERS: AND IT'S JUST BREAD AND WATER IN THE BIG DOLLHOUSE

Finally Jackie Hoffman suggested what is now in the show. Thanks Jackie, and, no, no royalties!

There's no First and Main in Baltimore, but it's a classic corner for hookers to hang out on.

. . . And "First and Main" rhymes with "complain"!

VELMA
EEK, CALL MY SHYSTERS,
LIPSHITZ AND STRAUSS
I GOTTA GET SPRUNG
FROM THE BIG DOLLHOUSE

ALL
BIG HOUSE!

LITTLE INEZ
NO FAIR

EDNA
NO FOOD

PENNY
NO FUN

ALL
BIG HOUSE!

MOTORMOUTH
AND OUR FIGHT HAS JUST BEGUN
'CAUSE IT'S FREEDOM'S FLAME
THAT SHE'D LIKE TO DOUSE
SO WE MUST BREAK OUT OF THIS

ALL
BIG DOLLHOUSE

MATRON
You do the crime, you gotta do the time.

TRACY
PENNY, I CAN'T TAKE ALL THIS WAITING
I'VE LOST MY MAN
PLUS MY HAIR'S DEFLATING!

PENNY
WELL, TRACY,
I HATE TO GRUMBLE OR GROUSE

ALL (screaming)
BUT IT'S YOUR FAULT THAT WE'RE IN
THIS BIG DOLLHOUSE!!

This is all that remains of Pia Zadora's character from the movie. In one early draft she helped TRACY and LINK escape from jail.

BEATNIK CHICK
HEY, COOL IT, LADIES
NO NEED TO SHOUT
AND DON'TCHA GOT AN OLD MAN
TO BAIL YOU OUT?

VELMA
HA! HER DADDY'S A LOSER,
A PERVERT, A SOUSE!

EDNA
WELL, IT'S JUST US GIRLS
IN THE BIG DOLLHOUSE

ALL
BIG HOUSE!

AMBER
GOD, I'M TOO YOUNG TO FRY!

ALL
BIG HOUSE!

EDNA
I'M BUSTING OUT!

MOTORMOUTH
GIRL, SO AM I!

ALL
LADY JUSTICE, HEAR MY PLEA
'CAUSE THE BIG DOLLHOUSE
THE BIG DOLLHOUSE
THE BIG DOLLHOUSE
AIN'T BIG ENOUGH FOR ME
FOR ME
FOR ME

A tribute to Gypsy.

EDNA
FOR ME!
(The song ends.)

The MATRON does some nifty Cab Calloway-esque call-and-response riffs in the musical segue.

Tensions run high among the jailed women, especially when AMBER and VELMA are released through their powerful connections. WILBUR shows up to post bail for everyone else (he's mortgaged the Har-De-Har Hut), but powerful VELMA's made sure TRACY will be held in solitary confinement until after the Miss Hairspray contest. It looks hopeless for TRACY, but even alone in the darkness she resolves to keep trying.

REPRISE: "GOOD MORNING BALTIMORE"

DRAMATIC THEORY: A brassy song reprised quietly is a revelation.

TRACY
OH, OH, OH
I'M ALL ALONE
MY HEART HAS GROWN BUT IT'S BROKEN, TOO

THIS MORNING LIFE WAS A
BALTIMORE FAIRY TALE
NOW I CAN'T MAKE BAIL!

MY MOTHER'S IN SHOCK
MY FATHER'S IN HOCK
I MUCH PREFER LINK'S ARMS
TO JAILHOUSE CELLS

SO, LINK, PLEASE
RESCUE ME NOW
'CAUSE I LOVE YOU
AND THIS PRISON SMELLS
LINK, HEAR THE BELLS!

AND GET READY BALTIMORE
THERE'S A BRIGHT, BRAND-NEW DAY IN STORE
LET ME OUT SO THIS DREAM'S UNFURLED
I'LL EAT SOME BREAKFAST,
THEN CHANGE THE WORLD!

AND I PROMISE BALTIMORE
ONCE I CHA-CHA RIGHT OUT OF THAT DOOR
THE WORLD'S GONNA WAKE UP AND SEE
LINK'S IN LOVE WITH ME!

HAR-DE-HAR HUT

Back at home, EDNA despairs that her daughter is in jail and there's nothing she can do about it. WILBUR, who's working on a secret invention to help TRACY, tries to comfort EDNA, but it's no easy task. She feels helpless and, for the first time in her life, old.

If EDNA was born in 1928, say, she'd have been a bobby-soxer in the mid-'40s.

EDNA

No, Wilbur. My time's come and gone. I'm a worn out pair of bobby sox, and the elastic's all stretched. Oh, Wilbur, I suddenly feel so old.

WILBUR

(MUSIC)
Nonsense, doll. You're as spry as a slinky. Whenever I'm near you it's like grabbing hold of a giant joy buzzer.

"YOU'RE TIMELESS TO ME"

WILBUR
*STYLES KEEP A CHANGIN'
THE WORLD'S REARRANGIN'
BUT EDNA, YOU'RE TIMELESS TO ME
HEMLINES ARE SHORTER
A BEER COSTS A QUARTER
BUT TIME CANNOT TAKE WHAT COMES FREE*

*YOU'RE LIKE A STINKY OLD CHEESE, BABE
JUST GETTIN' RIPER WITH AGE
YOU'RE LIKE A FATAL DISEASE, BABE
BUT THERE'S NO CURE
SO LET THIS FEVER RAGE*

*SOME FOLKS CAN'T STAND IT
SAY TIME IS A BANDIT
BUT I TAKE THE OPPOSITE VIEW
CAUSE WHEN I NEED A LIFT
TIME BRINGS A GIFT
ANOTHER DAY WITH YOU*

*A TWIST OR A WALTZ
IT'S ALL THE SAME SCHMALTZ
WITH JUST A CHANGE IN THE SCENERY
YOU'LL NEVER BE OLD HAT
THAT'S THAT!
OOH, OOH, YOU'RE TIMELESS TO ME*

EDNA
*FAD'S KEEP A-FADIN'
AND CASTRO'S INVADIN'
BUT WILBUR, YOU'RE TIMELESS TO ME*

*HAIRDOS ARE HIGHER
MINE FEELS LIKE BARBED WIRE
BUT YOU SAY I'M CHIC AS CAN BE!*

*YOU'RE LIKE A RARE VINTAGE RIPPLE
A VINTAGE THEY'LL NEVER FORGET
SO POUR ME A TEENY WEENIE TRIPLE
AND WE CAN TOAST THE FACT WE AIN'T DEAD YET!*

We wanted to write a love song, but to make it John Waters-y we decided to do it using back-handed compliments. When John first heard it, he teared up, which is quite a sight! And, besides the show-biz heaven of watching Harvey and Dick perform this number, we were doubly blessed to have our pal Nathan Lane sing the demo. Both roles!! He literally learned it after hearing it only once, which is why we call him our "Musical Comedy Rain Man." Harvey Fierstein, Dick Latessa, and two Nathan Lanes . . . whoever plays these parts in years to come has BIG shoes to fill!!

We had Steve Lawrence and Eydie Gorme in our heads when we wrote this. Hope they record it someday.

EDNA (cont'd)
I CAN'T STOP EATING
YOUR HAIRLINE'S RECEDING
AND SOON THERE'LL BE NOTHING AT ALL
SO YOU'LL WEAR A WIG
WHILE I ROAST A PIG
HEY! PASS THAT GERITOL®

GLENN MILLER HAD CLASS
THAT CHUBBY CHECKER'S A GAS
BUT THEY ALL PASS EVENTUALLY

YOU'LL NEVER BE PASSE
HIP HOORAY!
YOU'RE TIMELESS TO ME
(dance break)

EDNA
YOU'RE LIKE A BROKEN DOWN CHEVY
ALL YOU NEED IS A FRESH COAT OF PAINT

WILBUR
AND, EDNA, YOU GOT ME GOIN' HOT AND HEAVY
YOU'RE FAT AND OLD, BUT BABY, BORING YOU AIN'T!

WILBUR & EDNA
SOME FOLKS DON'T GET IT
BUT WE NEVER FRET IT
'CAUSE WE KNOW THAT TIME IS OUR FRIEND

AND IT'S PLAIN TO SEE
THAT YOU'RE STUCK WITH ME
UNTIL THE BITTER END

AND WE GOT A KID
WHO'S BLOWIN' THE LID
OFF THE TURNBLAD FAMILY TREE

EDNA
YOU'LL ALWAYS HIT THE SPOT
BIG SHOT!
YOU'RE TIMELESS TO ME

This is the most vaudevillian, old-time turn in the show.

Slogan: "For iron-poor blood!"

YOUR TWIST PARTY
WITH THE KING OF TWIST
CHUBBY CHECKER

DANCE! DANCE! DANCE! P 7007
PARKWAY

AS SEEN ON DICK CLARK'S AMERICAN BANDSTAND
AS FEATURED ON THE ED SULLIVAN SHOW
AS FEATURED IN TIME MAGAZINE

It Happened Last Night

VARIETY
NEW TWIST IN CAFE SOCIETY
ADULTS NOW DIG JUVES' NEW BEAT

Libretto
128

WILBUR
YOU'LL ALWAYS BE DU JOUR
MON AMOUR
YOU'RE TIMELESS TO ME

EDNA
YOU'LL ALWAYS BE FIRST STRING

A Sinatra Rat-Pack-ism.

WILBUR
RING-A-DING-DING!

WILBUR & EDNA
YOU'RE TIMELESS TO ME

EDNA
YOU'RE TIMELESS TO ME

He ends on a high note, she on a low note—comedy switcheroo in action!

WILBUR
YOU'RE TIMELESS TO ME

WILBUR & EDNA
YOU'RE TIMELESS TO ME!!

REPRISE: "TIMELESS TO ME"

WILBUR & EDNA
YOU NEED A FRESH COAT OF PLASTER

EDNA
BUT, WILBUR, I'M STILL HOT TO TROT

WILBUR
YEAH, EDNA, YOU'RE LIKE THE HINDENBURG DISASTER

EDNA
I'M FULL OF GAS!

WILBUR
BUT YOU WON'T BE FORGOT!!

John Cameron Swayze's slogan for Timex.

WILBUR & EDNA
LOVE TAKE A LICKIN'
BUT WE KEEP ON TICKIN'
WE'RE JUST LIKE THE CLOCK ON THE WALL

WILBUR
YEAH OUR SPRINGS NEVER POP

EDNA
AND ON THE DAY THAT YOU DROP

WILBUR & EDNA
WHOO! I'LL CATCH YOU WHEN YOU FALL

AND WE GOT A KID
WHO'S DONE WHAT SHE DID
AND WE'RE AS PROUD AS PROUD CAN BE

WILBUR
YOU'RE STILL MY BIG AFFAIR

EDNA
MEIN HERR!

WILBUR & EDNA
YOU'RE TIMELESS TO ME

EDNA
YOU'RE ROUNDING THIRD BASE NOW

WILBUR
HOLY COW!
YOU'RE TIMELESS TO ME

EDNA
I'LL ALWAYS CALL YOU HOME

WILBUR
SHABBAT SHALOM!

WILBUR & EDNA
YOU'RE TIMELESS TO ME
YOU'RE TIMELESS TO ME
YOU'RE TIMELESS TO ME
YOU'RE TIMELESS TO ME!!!

The "Shabbat Shalom" lyric is probably the best non sequitur joke we'll ever get in a song. You should have heard the "crickets" in Seattle after this line! But, oy, do the New York matinee crowds love it!!

Technically the TURNBLADS aren't Jewish, but comedy professionals tend to become Jewish.

This number stopped the show so we wrote several reprises. This one is still in the trunk.

WILBUR
YOU'RE LIKE SOME DUSTY OLD PAINTING
HELL, YOU'LL BE WORTH EVEN MORE WHEN YOU'RE DEAD

EDNA
AND, WILBUR, FABIAN HAS TEENYBOPPERS FAINTING
BUT HE'S TOO SCRAWNY
GIVE ME MIDDLE-AGE SPREAD!

BOTH
WE'RE FULL OF PASSION
BUT IT AIN'T FOR FASHION
'CAUSE WHO HAS THE TIME TO STAY HIP

THE ROAD'S HAD SOME BUMPS
BUT EVEN WITH LUMPS
IT'S SUCH A LOVELY TRIP

(YEAH,) THERE'S FIGHTS AND THERE'S FEUDS
BUT OUR LOVE INCLUDES
THE SIMPLE LIFETIME GUARANTEE

WILBUR
YOU'RE ALWAYS FIRST IN LINE

EDNA
HOW DIVINE!

BOTH
YOU'RE TIMELESS TO ME

EDNA
AS AVA GARDNER WOULD SAY

WILBUR
OLÉ

BOTH
YOU'RE TIMELESS TO ME

EDNA
THEY AIN'T SEEN NOTHIN' YET!

WILBUR
CIGARETTE?

BOTH
YOU'RE TIMELESS TO ME

EDNA
YOU'RE TIMELESS TO ME

WILBUR
YOU'RE TIMELESS TO ME

BOTH
YOU'RE TIMELESS TO ME!!!

131

Late that night LINK sneaks into the jail to apologize to TRACY. He also realizes he's in love with her, and gives her his Council ring. She's behind bars but she's never been happier.

TRACY

It's beautiful.
(She puts on the ring.)
I have a good life: great parents, my own room, stacks of 45s, three sweaters, plus a learner's permit good through August. But you know what I've been missing, Link?

LINK

I think I do.
(They try to kiss.)
Trace, they can keep us from kissing, but they can't stop us from singing.

"WITHOUT LOVE"

LINK

ONCE I WAS A SELFISH FOOL
WHO NEVER UNDERSTOOD
I NEVER LOOKED INSIDE MYSELF
THOUGH ON THE OUTSIDE, I LOOKED GOOD!

THEN WE MET AND YOU MADE ME
THE MAN I AM TODAY
TRACY, I'M IN LOVE WITH YOU
NO MATTER WHAT YOU WEIGH

LINK	**BACKUP**
'CAUSE WITHOUT LOVE	WITHOUT LOVE
LIFE IS LIKE THE SEASONS	
WITH NO SUMMER	OOH-OOH
WITHOUT LOVE	WITHOUT LOVE
LIFE IS ROCK 'N' ROLL WITHOUT A DRUMMER	OOH-OOH-OOH
TRACY, I'LL BE YOURS FOREVER	I'LL BE YOURS FOREVER
'CAUSE I NEVER WANNA BE	
WITHOUT LOVE	WITHOUT LOVE
SO TRACY, NEVER SET ME FREE	. . . DOOT

Our inspirations here were the great Marvin Gaye/Tammi Terrell duets of Motown. Unfortunately, they were actually recorded in '67/'68, a few years past Hairspray's time range. Buuuuuuut, since the young characters in our show are "forward thinkers," we took the liberty of writing a song that is a tad anachronistic. Here's to artistic license!!

LINK (cont'd)	BACKUP (cont'd)
NO, I AIN'T LYIN'	DOOT DO DOOT DO
NEVER SET ME FREE TRACY,	DOOT DO DOOT DO
NO, NO, NO!	NO, NO, NO!

TRACY	
ONCE I WAS A SIMPLE GIRL	AAH
THEN STARDOM CAME TO ME	AAH
BUT I WAS STILL A NOTHING	AAH-AAH
THOUGH A THOUSAND FANS MAY DISAGREE	AAH-AAH
FAME WAS JUST A PRISON	TRACY!
SIGNING AUTOGRAPHS A BORE	
I DIDN'T HAVE A CLUE	
'TIL YOU CAME BANGING ON MY DOOR	

THAT WITHOUT LOVE	. . . WITHOUT LOVE
LIFE IS LIKE MY DAD WITHOUT HIS BROMO	OOH-OOH
WITHOUT LOVE	WITHOUT LOVE
LIFE'S JUST MAKING OUT TO PERRY COMO	OOH-OOH-OOH

Perry Como was easy listenin', to put it mildly.

DARLING, I'LL BE YOURS FOREVER	I'LL BE YOURS FOREVER
'CAUSE I NEVER WANNA BE	
WITHOUT LOVE	WITHOUT LOVE

SO DARLING, THROW AWAY THE KEY

LINK & TRACY	
I'M YOURS FOREVER	DOOT DOOT DO DOOT
	DOOT DOOT DOOT

TRACY	
THROW AWAY THE KEY	DOOT DOO DOOT DOOT

LINK & TRACY	
YEAH, YEAH, YEAH!	YEAH, YEAH, YEAH!

(The lights dim on the jail and brighten on PENNY's bedroom. PRUDY is tying PENNY to the bed.)

PRUDY

Penny Lou Pingleton, you are absolutely, positively, permanently punished. This one's for being willful. This one's for being deceitful. This one's for being neglectful. And this one's for crying, "Wee wee wee, all the way home."
(The phone rings.)

This replaced:
"This one's for being peevish.
This one's for being petulant.
This one's for being persnickety."

PRUDY (cont'd)

Why is it every time you tie your daughter up, the
phone rings?
(PRUDY exits just as SEAWEED appears in the window.)

SEAWEED

Psst! Penny!

PENNY

Seaweed! Shhh! Don't let my mother hear you.

SEAWEED

What happened?

PENNY

She's punishing me for going to jail without her permission.

SEAWEED

I've come to rescue the fair maiden from her tower.

PENNY

Oh, Seaweed, you do care! I was worried it was just a lonely
teenager's forbidden fantasy.

SEAWEED

From the first moment I saw you I knew that even the
colors of our skin couldn't keep us apart.
(struggling with the rope)
But, damn, these knots are something else.

PENNY

Hurry, Seaweed!

SEAWEED

LIVING IN THE GHETTO
BLACK IS EVERYWHERE YA GO
WHO'D'VE THOUGHT I'D LOVE A GIRL
WITH SKIN AS WHITE AS WINTER'S SNOW

PENNY

IN MY IVORY TOWER
LIFE WAS JUST A HOSTESS SNACK
BUT NOW I'VE TASTED CHOCOLATE
AND I'M NEVER GOING BACK

(SEAWEED sets PENNY free.)

In an earlier draft, SEAWEED envisions a better future, called "The Really, Really Good Society."

replaced: "Our skins may be black and white, but our passion will always be purple!"

PENNY & SEAWEED   **BACKUP**
'CAUSE WITHOUT LOVE   . . . WITHOUT LOVE

SEAWEED
LIFE IS LIKE A BEAT THAT YOU CAN'T FOLLOW   OOH-OOH

PENNY & SEAWEED
WITHOUT LOVE   WITHOUT LOVE

PENNY
LIFE IS DORIS DAY AT THE APOLLO   OOH-OOH

PENNY & SEAWEED
DARLING, I'LL BE YOURS FOREVER   I'LL BE YOURS FOREVER
'CAUSE I NEVER WANNA BE
WITHOUT LOVE   WITHOUT LOVE

SEAWEED
DARLING, NEVER SET ME FREE

SEAWEED & PENNY
I'M YOURS FOREVER   DOOT DOOT DOO DOOT
NEVER SET ME FREE   DOOT DOOT DOO DOOT
NO, NO, NO!   NO, NO, NO!

(*The light comes on in the jail again. From now on we can see both* COUPLES *at once.*)

✂ CUT

PENNY: But where can we go?
SEAWEED: I don't know. Wilmington?
PENNY: That's just a crazy dream!

LINK   **BACKUP**
IF YOU'RE LOCKED UP IN THIS PRISON, TRACE   OOH-OOH
I DON'T KNOW WHAT I'LL DO   OOH-OOH

TRACY
LINK, I'VE GOT TO BREAK OUT   OOH-OOH
SO THAT I CAN GET MY HANDS ON YOU   I CAN GET MY HANDS ON YOU

SEAWEED
GIRL, IF I CAN'T TOUCH YOU NOW   OOH, OOH, OOH, OOH
I'M GONNA LOSE CONTROL   LOSE CONTROL

PENNY
SEAWEED, YOU'RE MY BLACK WHITE KNIGHT   BLACK WHITE KNIGHT
I'VE FOUND MY BLUE-EYED SOUL

SEAWEED
SWEET FREEDOM IS OUR GOAL

BACKUP
SWEET FREEDOM IS OUR GOAL

LINK
TRACE, I WANNA KISS YA!

TRACY
THEN I CAN'T WAIT FOR PAROLE . . .

Oh Link, I've got to get out of here. If we only had some hairspray and a Zippo lighter, I think we can make an EZ-Bake oven kind of blowtorch!

LINK
Well, I've got a Zippo lighter! And, uh . . .
(embarrassed)
I've got some hairspray, too.
(He produces it from his jacket.)

TRACY
Link, what a special night! Your ring! And our very own blowtorch!
(As the number continues, LINK torches the cell bars to make a large TRACY-shaped opening through which she escapes.)

LINK
Oh, Tracy!

TRACY
Oh, Link!

PENNY
Oh, Seaweed!

SEAWEED
Oh, Penny!

PRUDY
(enters and sees SEAWEED and PENNY on the bed)
Oh my God! Colored people in the house. I'll never sell it now!

ALL
'CAUSE WITHOUT LOVE

SEAWEED
LIFE IS LIKE A PROM THAT WON'T INVITE US

BACKUP
OOH-OOH

COMEDY THEORY:
Incongruous items together.

Mercenary echoes of Shylock in The Merchant of Venice, when his daughter runs off with his money: "My daughter! O my ducats!"

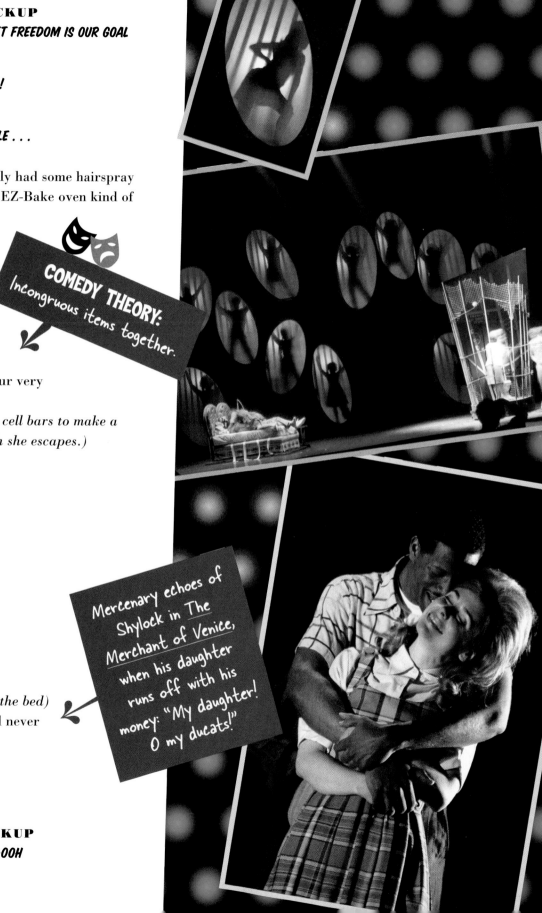

ALL
WITHOUT LOVE

LINK   **BACKUP**
LIKE GETTING MY BIG BREAK AND LARYNGITIS *OOH-OOH*

ALL
WITHOUT LOVE

PENNY   **BACKUP**
LIFE'S A 45 WHEN YOU CAN'T BUY IT   *OOH-OOH*

ALL
WITHOUT LOVE

TRACY   **BACKUP**
LIFE IS LIKE MY MOTHER ON A DIET   *OOH-OOH-OOH*

ALL
LIKE A WEEK THAT'S ONLY MONDAYS
ONLY ICE CREAM NEVER SUNDAES
LIKE A CIRCLE WITH NO CENTER
LIKE A DOOR MARKED "DO NOT ENTER"!
DARLING, I'LL BE YOURS FOREVER
'CAUSE I NEVER WANNA BE
WITHOUT LOVE

PENNY & LINK   **BACKUP**
YES NOW YOU'VE CAPTURED ME

                                                        WITHOUT LOVE

SEAWEED & TRACY
I SURRENDER HAPPILY

                                                        WITHOUT LOVE - OOH

LINK
SO DARLING

ALL
NEVER SET ME FREE

                                                        DOOT DOOT DOOT DOOT
                                                        DOOT DOOT DOOT DOOT

ALL
DARLING, YOU HAD BEST BELIEVE ME,
NEVER LEAVE ME WITHOUT LOVE!

It's almost midnight, it's raining hard, and escapees TRACY and LINK seek refuge at MOTORMOUTH's record shop, where all the black kids, as well as SEAWEED and run-away PENNY, have gathered. MOTOR-MOUTH tries to rally the group to start planning an assault on the Miss Hairspray special, but after all they've been through, the group is understandably discouraged.

"The Lord never said Win. The Lord said Try."

TRACY
Anyway, this time it won't be like Mother-Daughter Day again. Mrs. Von Tussle said there'll be armed guards at the Eventorium.

PENNY
With arms.

TRACY
Someone could get shot.

GILBERT
And for what? Just so we can dance on some ofay show?

Lesser-known slang for "honky."

MOTORMOUTH
Hold it! Nobody ever said this was gonna be easy. If something's worth having, it's worth fighting for. Tracy, why did you start all this in the first place? Was it just to dance on TV?

TRACY

No.

MOTORMOUTH

Was it so you could get the boy?

TRACY

No, I almost lost him because of it.

MOTORMOUTH

Then maybe it was just to get yourself famous.

TRACY

(taking exception, slightly)
No. I just think it's stupid we can't all dance together.

MOTORMOUTH

So you tried once and you failed. We can't get lazy when things get crazy.
Children, you were not the first to try and you won't be the last, but I am
here to tell you that I'm gonna keep lining up until someday somebody
breaks through. And I've been looking at that door a lot longer than you.

TRACY

What door?

MOTORMOUTH

The front door.

"I KNOW WHERE I'VE BEEN"

MOTORMOUTH
THERE'S A LIGHT IN THE DARKNESS
THOUGH THE NIGHT IS BLACK AS MY SKIN
THERE'S A LIGHT BURNING BRIGHT
SHOWING ME THE WAY
BUT I KNOW WHERE I'VE BEEN

THERE'S A CRY IN THE DISTANCE
IT'S A VOICE THAT COMES FROM DEEP WITHIN
THERE'S A CRY ASKING WHY
I PRAY THE ANSWER'S UP AHEAD
'CAUSE I KNOW WHERE I'VE BEEN

	BACKUP
THERE'S A ROAD WE'VE BEEN TRAVELIN'	00-00
LOST SO MANY ON THE WAY	00-00
BUT THE RICHES WILL BE PLENTY	00-00
WORTH THE PRICE WE HAD TO PAY	00-00

CUT

"Yesterday is what tomorrow is standing on."

MOTORMOUTH	BACKUP
THERE'S A DREAM IN THE FUTURE	. . . DREAM, OO-OO
THERE'S A STRUGGLE WE HAVE YET TO WIN	
AND THERE'S PRIDE IN MY HEART	HOO-OO
'CAUSE I KNOW WHERE I'M GOING	HOO-OO-OO-OO
AND I KNOW WHERE I'VE BEEN	
THERE'S A ROAD WE MUST TRAVEL	THERE'S A ROAD WE MUST TRAVEL
THERE'S A PROMISE WE MUST MAKE	THERE'S A PROMISE WE MUST MAKE
'CAUSE THE RICHES WILL BE PLENTY	'CAUSE THE RICHES WILL BE PLENTY
WORTH THE RISK AND THE CHANCES	WORTH THE RISK AND THE CHANCES
THAT WE TAKE	THAT WE TAKE
THERE'S A DREAM IN THE FUTURE	. . . DREAM, HOO-OO-OO
THERE'S A STRUGGLE	
WE HAVE YET TO WIN	STRUGGLE
USE THAT PRIDE	HOO-OO-OO
IN OUR HEARTS	PRIDE
	IN OUR HEARTS
TO LIFT US TO TOMORROW	LIFT US UP
'CAUSE JUST TO SIT STILL WOULD BE A SIN	OO-OO-OO-OO
OOH . . . SIT STILL	
I KNOW IT, I KNOW IT	
I KNOW WHERE I'M	
GOIN'	
LORD KNOWS	
I KNOW WHERE I'VE BEEN	
	OH WHEN WE WIN
I'LL GIVE THANKS TO MY GOD	I'LL GIVE THANKS TO MY GOD
'CAUSE I KNOW WHERE I'VE BEEN	'CAUSE I KNOW WHERE I'VE BEEN

"If you're not part of the solution, you're part of the problem."—Eldridge Cleaver

"I KNOW WHERE I'VE BEEN"

This was one of the first songs Scott and I wrote, inspired by a scene late in the movie that takes place on the black side of town. It never dawned on us that a torrent of protest would follow us from almost everyone involved with the show. "It's too sad. . . . It's too preachy. . . . It doesn't belong. . . . Tracy should sing the eleven o'clock number." We simply didn't want our show to be yet another show-biz version of a civil rights story where the black characters are just background. And what could be more Tracy Turnblad-like than to give the "eleven o'clock number" to the black family at the heart of the struggle? Luckily, although the intelligentsia remained aloof, the audiences embraced this moment, which enriches the happy ending to follow, and it is our proudest achievement of the entire experience of writing Hairspray.

MOTORMOUTH
(TO TRACY)
ARE YOU GONNA LET SOME
WASHED-UP BONEY ASS
TELL YOU WHAT TO DO?

(TO LINK)
ARE YOU GONNA LET SOME
STUCK UP BEAUTY QUEEN
MAKE A MOUSE OF YOU?

(TO PENNY)
AND ARE YOU GONNA LOSE
THIS SWEET SWEET MAN
CAUSE PEOPLE ARE ACTING CRAZED?

(TO SEAWEED)
AND SPEAKING OF MEN,
DID YOU JUST SAY QUIT?
THAT'S NOT THE BOY I RAISED

I TAUGHT HIM TO
STEP ON UP TO THE HIGHER GROUND
STEP ON UP AND SHOUT
STEP ON UP AND TELL THE WORLD
JUST WHAT YOU'RE ALL ABOUT

I TAUGHT HIM TO
STEP ON UP AND THEN TURN AROUND
AND GRAB SOMEBODY'S HAND
AND HELP 'EM STEP ON UP
STEP ON UP, STEP ON UP

LITTLE INEZ
I AIN'T LETTIN NO
OFAY COUNCIL
TELL ME WHEN I CAN DANCE

LINK
I DON'T CARE
ABOUT STARDOM NOW
I'VE FOUND MY TRUE ROMANCE

TRACEY
I AIN'T STOPPIN
'TIL ALL MY FRIENDS
ARE STANDING NEXT TO ME

SEAWEED
AND I CAN'T FORGET
WHAT MY MAMA SAID
"SOMEDAY, WE'LL ALL BE FREE!"

SHE TAUGHT ME TO
STEP ON UP TO THE HIGHER GROUND
STEP ON UP AND SHOUT
STEP ON UP AND TELL ALL THE WORLD
JUST WHAT YOU'RE ALL ABOUT

MOTORMOUTH
YES, I TAUGHT HIM TO
STEP ON UP AND THEN TURN AROUND
AND GRAB SOMEBODY'S HAND
AND HELP 'EM STEP ON UP
STEP ON UP, STEP ON UP
GO ON, STEP ON UP
STEP ON UP, STEP ON UP

MOTORMOUTH
'CAUSE THERE'S A ROAD WE'VE BEEN TRAV-
ELIN'
LOST SO MANY ON THE WAY
BUT THE RICHES WILL BE PLENTY

ALL
WORTH THE PRICE WE HAD TO PAY!!!

(BREAK)

I TAUGHT HIM TO
STEP ON UP AND THEN TURN AROUND
AND GRAB SOMEBODY'S HAND
AND HELP 'EM STEP ON UP
STEP ON UP, STEP ON UP
GO ON, STEP ON UP
STEP ON UP, STEP ON UP

STEP ON UP TO THE HIGHER GROUND
STEP ON UP AND SHOUT
STEP ON UP AND TELL THE WORLD
JUST WHAT YOU'RE ALL ABOUT

I TAUGHT HIM TO
STEP ON UP AND THEN TURN AROUND
AND GRAB SOMEBODY'S HAND
AND HELP 'EM STEP ON UP
STEP ON UP, STEP ON UP

William at Work

William Ivey Long, Costume Designer

When designing costumes, you don't want to just fling finished sketches in front of a director and choreographer (what hubris!). Instead, I prefer to do several different sweeps: first, the thumbnail sketches of all the characters in the show, rendered roughly about two-and-a-half inches tall, with some color; second, the Rauschenberg-esque collage sweep (made from period catalogs and vintage photographs all over-painted, switched, and shifted) showing all of the characters in each scene attached in a line, the principals at center, so you can see what the whole scene looks like (this is what you see here—for the finale); finally, the finished full-size grown-up costume renderings (except that sometimes I don't finish all of these, oops).

"Can't Stop the Beat"
Saturday night – Baltimore Eventorium

2117 COUNCIL MEMBER
Jennifer Gambatese

1517 COUNCIL MEMBER
Peter Matthew Smith (?)

1417 COUNCIL MEMBER
John Hill

1617 COUNCIL MEMBER
Adam Fleming

2217 COUNCIL MEMBER
Katherine Leonard

1717 COUNCIL MEMBER
Todd Michael Smith

2317 COUNCIL MEMBER
Hollie Howard

0317 WILBUR TURNBLAD
Dick Latessa

0217 EDNA TURNBLAD
Harvey Fierstein

0117 TRACY TURNBLAD
Marissa Winokur

0417 LINK LARKIN
Matthew Morrison

1117 PENNY PINGLETON
Kerry Butler

0917 SEAWEED
Corey Reynolds

2917 COUNCIL MEMBER
Greg Graham

3217A COUNCIL MEMBER
Brooke Tansley

3017A MR. SPRITZER
Joel Vig

1317 PRUDY PINGLETON
Jackie Hoffman

1217 GOVERNOR
Joel Vie

1017 LITTLE INEZ
Danelle Wilson

0817 MOTORMOUTH MABEL
Mary Bond Davis

0717 VELMA VON TASSLE
Linda Hart

0617 AMBER VON TUSSLE
Laura Bell Bundy

0517 CORNY COLLINS
Clarke Thorell

FSD7
e Greaves

3017B MALE SWING
Joshua Bergasse

2817 FSD8
Judine Richard

3217B FEMALE SWING
Sabrina Scherff

2417 COUNCIL MEMBER
Shoshana Bean

2517 FSD5
Kamilah Martin

1817 MSD5
Eric Anthony

1917 MSD6
Kashad Naylor

2617 FSD6
Shayna Steele

2017 MSD7
Eric Dysart

Act Two
SCENE 5

(The Baltimore Eventorium. Lights and music herald The Corny Collins Spectacular. A Miss Teenage Hairspray 1962 scoreboard shows AMBER leading TRACY by a few votes. Drum roll . . . CORNY appears on stage.)

After "I Know Where I've Been," this phony, glitzy Vegas blast is meant to be a fun jolt.

Designer/architect David Rockwell liked this joke.

CORNY
(MUSIC)
And now, live from the certified up-to-code Baltimore Eventorium . . . for the first time ever on nationwide television . . . it's The Corny Collins Spectacular . . .

COUNCIL MEMBERS
HE'S CORNY!

CORNY
. . . brought to you by Ultra Clutch Hairspray!

Libretto

"What Gives a Girl Power and Punch." Whoops, an inadvertent homage to "Mack & Mabel" ("What gives a man power and punch?"). . . . Thanks, Jerry Herman!

From the Rat Pack era, when women were dames, broads, birds, skirts, chicks, and babes.

OLD JOKE: HUSBAND, UPSTAIRS: Has the milkman come yet? WIFE, DOWNSTAIRS: No, but he's breathing hard!

CORNY
WHAT GIVES A GIRL
POWER AND PUNCH?
IS IT CHARM, IS IT POISE?
NO, IT'S HAIRSPRAY!

WHAT GETS A GAL
ASKED OUT TO LUNCH?
IS IT BRAINS, IS IT DOUGH?
NO, IT'S HAIRSPRAY!

IF YOU TAKE A RIDE
WITH NO CAN AT YOUR SIDE
THEN YOUR FLIP WILL BE GONE WITH THE WIND

BUT IF YOU SPRAY IT AND LOCK IT,
YOU CAN TAKE OFF IN A ROCKET
AND IN OUTER SPACE
EACH HAIR WILL BE IN PLACE

WHY TAKE A CHANCE
WHEN YOU GET UP AND DANCE?
IF YOU TWIST, I INSIST
YOU USE HAIRSPRAY

AND TELL YOUR MOTHER
HER HEAD SHE SHOULD SMOTHER
WITH ULTRA CLUTCH FAITHFULLY
FAITHFULLY

BACKUP
. . . HAIRSPRAY!

. . . HAIRSPRAY!

OOH
OO-OO-OOH-OOH
THEN YOUR FLIP
OOH-OOH-OOH!

YOU CAN TAKE OFF IN A ROCKET
. . . OUTER SPACE
HAIR WILL BE IN PLACE

OOH, OOH
OOH, OO-OO-OOH
OOH
. . . HAIRSPRAY!

OOH
OOH, OOH
ULTRA CLUTCH

ALL
SO IF YOU'RE A REDHEAD, A BLONDE OR BRUNETTE - WOO!

CORNY
JUST TAKE MY ADVICE
AND YOU MIGHT JUST GET
YOU MIGHT JUST
THE ONLY THING BETTER THAN HAIRSPRAY
THAT'S ME!
FORGET THE MILKMAN
THE ONLY THING BETTER THAN HAIRSPRAY

BACKUP

OOH, OOH . . . HAIRSPRAY
SKA-DOO-DL-E-YA DOO-DL-E-YA DO WAH

HAIRSPRAY WOW

CUT

CUT SONG: "Take a Spin" was replaced with "Hairspray." Originally the competition for Miss Hairspray was for Miss Auto Show, but cars onstage are very expensive.

"TAKE A SPIN"

CORNY
WRAP YOUR ARM
AROUND YOUR BABY
AND TAKE A SPIN

SELL THE FARM
LOSE THE KIDS
TURN YOUR GRANDPA IN

LUCKY YOU I SEE NOTHING
BUT CURVES UP AHEAD
NICE SOFT SHOULDERS
LOOK OUT FOR THOSE BOULDERS
YOU COULD WIND UP DEAD!

HER REAR VIEW'S
GOT ME THINKIN'
ABOUT CHANGING LANES

I'M TELLING YOU
YOU WON'T GET THIS ACTION
ON BOATS AND PLANES

BESIDES, THE *TITANIC* NEVER SHOWS UP
THE *HINDENBURG* BLOWS UP
THEN THEY'RE CONTACTING
YOUR NEXT OF KIN

SO GET BEHIND THE WHEEL
FILL 'ER UP, MAN, AND
MAKE HER SQUEAL
THE FUN WILL BEGIN ONCE YOU
TAKE A SPIN

Act Two, Scene 5

149

CORNY
THAT'S ME!

COUNCIL MEMBERS
AH, AH, AH, AH, AH, AH, AH, AH, AH
AH, AH, AH, AH, AH, AH, AH, AH, AH

CORNY & COUNCIL MEMBERS
WHAT MAKES A MAN
REACH OUT AND TOUCH?
ULTRA CLUTCH!

ALL
SO IF YOU'RE A REDHEAD, A BLONDE OR BRUNETTE

CORNY	**BACKUP**
JUST TAKE MY ADVICE	
AND YOU MIGHT JUST GET	*YOU MIGHT JUST*
THE ONLY THING BETTER THAN HAIRSPRAY	*OOH, OOH . . . HAIRSPRAY*
THAT'S ME!	*SKA-DOO-DL-E-YA DOO-DL-E-YA DO WAH*

GIRLS
HE'S CORNY COLLINS!

CORNY	**BACKUP**
THE ONLY THING BETTER THAN HAIRSPRAY	*HAIRSPRAY WOW!*
THAT'S ME!	

CORNY & THE COUNCILETTES
SKA-DOO-DL-E-YA-DO-WAH
SKA-DOO-DL-E-DOO-WAH-DO-WAH

CORNY
HEY BABY, YOU LOOK LIKE YOU COULD USE A STIFF ONE!

BRENDA
SKA-DOO-DL-DOO-DO-WAH!

(Applause. From the wings, a MAN in a hat, a fake nose, and a gigantic hairspray can walks onto the stage. VELMA approaches suspiciously.)

VELMA
And we're off for network commercial. What the hell is this?

MAN (WILBUR)
Product placement. The sponsor insists.

CORNY's a liberal, but he's also libidinous.

CLASSIC CON: The old shell game.

The windows of the Baltimore Eventorium recall the arched windows of Eero Saarinen's TWA Terminal.

VELMA

What a relief. We needed a little something there.
(suddenly shifting)
Say, don't I know you?

WILBUR

Honest, Velma, I'm a total stranger.
*(VELMA whips off his hat and funny glasses to reveal
WILBUR.)*

COMEDY THEORY:
Unwitting self-revelation.

VELMA

You!

WILBUR

Damn!

VELMA

(calling for backup)
Guard! Riot squad! I want everybody out of the lobby
and up here pronto.
*(SEAWEED and three MOTORMOUTH BOYS dressed as
GUARDS run in from the aisle.)*
Ha! What is this? Some kind of Trojan Horse? What's
inside, your jailbird daughter?

"A nonconformist, because
conformity didn't fit her!"

CUT

WILBUR

Not a chance.

MAGICIAN'S TACTIC:
Misdirection

VELMA

Well, if she's hiding in that can, she'll rot in that
can. Guard, if anybody so much as touches that
thing, . . . open fire!

MOTORMOUTH

(dressed as a guard wearing a riot helmet)
Understood, Ma'am.
(MOTORMOUTH pulls WILBUR off.)

WILBUR

You win this time, Von Tussle. You're one clever woman,
I'll say that.

VELMA

(to SEAWEED)
Get out!
(SEAWEED exits up the theater aisle.)
And coming back to Corny on camera one in 3 . . . 2 . . .

CORNY

And now for the talent portion of the competition, where the front-runner gals present a dance of their own creation. *(looking at the scoreboard)* Presently, Amber Von Tussle and Tracy Turnblad are neck and neck. But since, according to the latest police bulletins, Miss Turnblad is still at large . . .

AMBER

(leaning into the shot) At VERY large.

CORNY

. . . our Miss Hairspray might just be a foregone conclusion. Still, our rules say the contestant has to dance for it. Ready, Amber?

AMBER

Ready as a rabbit on Easter, Corny. Tracy Turnblad, this song is all about you.

replaced: "Ready as instant coffee, Corny!" Instant beverages were all the rage then.

"It's not too late to phone in your vote. Operators are sitting by!"

CUT

"I hope you are conscious and in front of the tube, because . . . "

"COOTIES"

AMBER
THEY CAME FROM WAY FAR OUT
IN OUTER SPACE
SHE'S HARD TO MISS
AND SO THEY LANDED ON HER FACE!

COUNCIL MEMBERS

OW-OOT

GUYS (GIRLS)
SHE'S GOT COOTIES (COOTIES)

AMBER
THEY'VE FOUND A PLACE TO NEST

GUYS (GIRLS)
SHE'S GOT COOTIES (COOTIES)

AMBER
IF I WERE HER I'D BE DEPRESSED
LONG TAILED, SHARP NAILED
FUZZY LEGS, LAYING EGGS

Libretto

AMBER

C'mon everybody, let's stamp them out!!

COUNCIL MEMBERS

SHE'S GOT COOTIES

AMBER

IN SCIENCE CLASS
SHE'S LIKE A WALKING SHOW-AND-TELL

COUNCIL MEMBERS

SHE'S GOT COOTIES

AMBER

YOU KNOW SHE'S COMING DOWN THE HALL
FROM JUST THE SMELL!

GUYS (GIRLS)

SHE'S GOT COOTIES (COOTIES)

AMBER

NOBODY WANTS TO SIT BY HER

GUYS (GIRLS)

SHE'S GOT COOTIES (COOTIES)

AMBER

DON'T NEED A COAT 'CAUSE SHE'S GOT FUR!
CIRCLE, CIRCLE, DOT, DOT, DOT

ALL

HURRY, GET YOUR COOTIE SHOT!

AMBER

DRESSES LIKE A CIRCUS CLOWN

COUNCIL MEMBERS

SOMEBODY OUGHTA HOSE HER DOWN

AMBER

GREW UP IN A COOTIE ZOO
I BET HER TWO-TON MAMA'S GOT 'EM TOO!
And that's for you!

AMBER

Thank you, ladies, gentlemen, and kids. I'm now ready to consume the title of Miss Teenage Hairspray.
(CORNY leads SPRITZER on. SPRITZER carries the crown and bouquet.)

She's that greedy.

CORNY

Just to be sure, I think we'd better check the board.

SPRITZER

Could we please see the tally?
(All turn to the scoreboard. The numbers spin and AMBER is the winner by a few votes.)

SPRITZER

Yes, Amber Von Tussle just squeaks in as the winner.

AMBER

What'd I tell you? Give me the crown, give me the flowers, and everybody start bowing!
(AMBER snatches the crown and slaps it onto her head. VELMA puts the Miss Teenage Hairspray 1962 sash on AMBER.)

TRACY

(from the theater aisle)
Not so fast, Amber. Look who's coming in the front door.
(an explosion of music and light)

CORNY

Right on schedule! I mean, I know nothing about this complex plan. Ladies and gentlemen, I give you the never-to-be-counted-out Tracy Turnblad!
(A spotlight picks up TRACY as she makes her way up the aisle, singing, dancing, and celebrating. She is followed by LINK, PENNY, SEAWEED, the BLACK FEMALE ENSEMBLE, and LITTLE INEZ.)

"YOU CAN'T STOP THE BEAT"

TRACY

YOU CAN'T STOP AN AVALANCHE
AS IT RACES DOWN THE HILL
YOU CAN TRY TO STOP THE SEASONS, GIRL
BUT CHA KNOW YOU NEVER WILL
AND YOU CAN TRY TO STOP MY DANCIN' FEET
BUT I JUST CANNOT STAND STILL

COMEDY THEORY:
Unwitting self-revelation.

CUT

" . . . direct from her recent appearance at the Baltimore House of Detention . . . "

Thank YOU, don't SUE!
"River Deep, Mountain High" meets "The Beat Goes On."

TRACY (cont'd)
'CAUSE THE WORLD KEEPS SPINNING
ROUND AND ROUND
AND MY HEART'S KEEPING TIME
TO THE SPEED OF SOUND
I WAS LOST 'TIL I HEARD THE DRUMS
THEN I FOUND MY WAY

TRACY & LINK
'CAUSE YOU CAN'T STOP THE BEAT

TRACY
EVER SINCE THIS OLD WORLD BEGAN
A WOMAN FOUND OUT IF SHE SHOOK IT
SHE COULD SHAKE UP A MAN
AND SO I'M GONNA SHAKE AND SHIMMY IT
THE BEST THAT I CAN TODAY

'CAUSE YOU CAN'T STOP
THE MOTION OF THE OCEAN
OR THE SUN IN THE SKY
YOU CAN WONDER IF YOU WANNA
BUT I NEVER ASK WHY

AND IF YOU TRY TO HOLD ME DOWN
I'M GONNA SPIT IN YOUR EYE AND SAY
THAT YOU CAN'T STOP THE BEAT!

What d'ya say, Penny?
(*PENNY appears. She is totally restyled COOL!
The remaining BLACK DANCERS escort her.*)

Yet another Cinderella!

PENNY	BACKUP
I am now a checkerboard chick!	

That is, black and white together.

YOU CAN'T STOP A RIVER	
AS IT RUSHES TO THE SEA	OOH-OOH
YOU CAN TRY AND STOP THE HANDS OF TIME	
BUT CHA KNOW IT JUST WON'T BE	
AND IF THEY TRY TO STOP US, SEAWEED	
I'LL CALL THE NAACP!	

PENNY

'CAUSE THE WORLD KEEPS SPINNING
ROUND AND ROUND

AND MY HEART'S KEEPING TIME
TO THE SPEED OF SOUND

SEAWEED

ROUND AND ROUND

SPEED OF SOUND

I WAS LOST 'TIL I HEARD THE DRUMS
THEN I FOUND MY WAY

PENNY, SEAWEED, TRACY & LINK
'CAUSE YOU CAN'T STOP THE BEAT

EVER SINCE WE FIRST SAW THE LIGHT
A MAN AND WOMAN LIKED TO SHAKE IT
ON A SATURDAY NIGHT
AND SO I'M GONNA SHAKE AND SHIMMY IT
WITH ALL MY MIGHT TODAY-AY-AY-AY

'CAUSE YOU CAN'T STOP
THE MOTION OF THE OCEAN
OR THE RAIN FROM ABOVE
THEY CAN TRY TO STOP THE PARADISE
WE'RE DREAMING OF
BUT THEY CANNOT STOP THE RHYTHM
OF TWO HEARTS IN LOVE TO STAY
'CAUSE YOU CAN'T STOP THE BEAT!

(The ARMED GUARDS begin to turn around to reveal themselves to be the BLACK MALE ENSEMBLE.)

TRACY
Get her!
(The BLACK MALE ENSEMBLE carries VELMA off.)
Amber, this is my dance, and it's dedicated to everybody!

(TRACY, LINK, SEAWEED, PENNY, and the BLACK KIDS dance their asses off then pull the COUNCIL MEMBERS in until all the KIDS are dancing together! All, that is, except AMBER, who has taken the crown and sash and defiantly taken possession of the throne.)

More Cinderella!

ALL
EVER SINCE WE FIRST SAW THE LIGHT
A MAN AND WOMAN LIKED TO SHAKE IT
ON A SATURDAY NIGHT
AND SO I'M GONNA SHAKE AND SHIMMY IT
WITH ALL MY MIGHT TODAY

'CAUSE YOU CAN'T STOP
THE MOTION OF THE OCEAN
OR THE RAIN FROM ABOVE
THEY CAN TRY TO STOP THE PARADISE
WE'RE DREAMING OF
BUT THEY CANNOT STOP THE RHYTHM
OF TWO HEARTS IN LOVE TO STAY
'CAUSE YOU CAN'T STOP THE BEAT!
YOU CAN'T STOP THE BEAT!!
YOU CAN'T STOP THE BEAT!!!

TRACY!

(triumphant applause)

CORNY

Everyone, look. . . . Look at the scoreboard!
*(ALL turn to see the scoreboard spontaneously
combusting, showing TRACY is the overwhelming winner.)*
Tracy Turnblad, I declare you Miss Teenage
Hairspray 1962!

VELMA & AMBER

NO!

AMBER

It's wrong! It's just so wrong!

LITTLE INEZ

(to AMBER)
Hand over that halo, honey.

AMBER

You'll have to rip it from my cold, dead hands.

LITTLE INEZ

That'll work.

TRACY

You can keep your stupid crown, Amber. I have my heart
set on something a lot more important.

Contrary to Cinderella, TRACY turns down the crown. She's too advanced for pageants now.

Ripping it from her "cold, dead scalp" was too grotesque.

157

LINK

Would that happen to be . . . me?

TRACY

Of course you, Link. But I also want a graduate degree in Musicology with a minor in Ethnic Studies. And I want to be the first one to say, *The Corny Collins Show* is now and forevermore officially integrated!
(A cheer fills the Eventorium.)

CORNY

America, look up! Here's history right before your eyes. Television will never be the same.

SPRITZER

(entering ecstatic, takes the mike from CORNY)
This is marvelous. The phones are going crazy. The whole country's watching. Even the Governor called. He's enjoying the show so much that he's granted a pardon to Tracy, plus a full scholarship to Essex Community College. You cannot buy this kind of publicity. Velma, you are a genius!

VELMA

I am? Yes, I am.

SPRITZER

Ultra Clutch is about to launch an entirely new line of products and I want this woman to head the campaign.

VELMA

(curiously)
I just don't know what to say.

SPRITZER

It comes with offices, a company car, and a multi-figured salary.

VELMA

(hopefully)
I just don't know what to say.

SPRITZER

Velma Von Tussle, you are the newly appointed vice president of Ultra Glow: beauty products for women of color!

ANACHRONISM WATCH: TRACY is the Voice of Tomorrow!!

CORNY's dreams come true: Cinderella time for a hipster!

John Waters gave us the name of a real but lousy-sounding local college.

In one draft, VELMA was arrested for payola (plugging records for bribes).

CUT

CORNY: "Velma, tolerance is something you'll just have to learn to tolerate!"

VELMA

(stupefied)
I just don't know what to say!

SPRITZER

(to LINK and TRACY)
And America would like to hear you two kids sing our new theme song. I think I can get you a recording contract.

LINK

My big break!
(The happiness is shattered with a scream as PRUDY runs down the aisle . . .)

PRUDY: This is the apocalypse!
EDNA: No, Prudy, it's the New Testament.

PRUDY

Give me back my daughter! I know you've got her. I saw it on TV.
(PENNY stops and faces PRUDY. SEAWEED stands protectively by.)
Penny. I hardly recognize you done up like that.

PENNY

I'm a pretty girl, Mama.

PRUDY

And you look so happy. I can't say it's what I want, but if this fine-looking, catlike black boy is responsible for the light in your eyes, then how could I object?
(PRUDY and PENNY embrace. SEAWEED embraces PRUDY.)

The line was originally "This big, strapping, sensuous, musky, full-lipped catlike black boy." Overkill, we decided.

CORNY

Live television—there's nothing like it.

LINK

This may not be the right moment since we're on national TV and all, but, Tracy, if I don't kiss you now I just may bust a gut.

TRACY

Well, I certainly wouldn't want you to hurt yourself.
(They kiss.)

Could i have the only improvised line on Broadway?

When PRUDY enters through the audience to reclaim her lost daughter, Jack (the director) had me crawl over the front row. I couldn't resist something snide—for god's sake, there was no damn room and I'm literally crawling over people—and it became the talk of the town, if you consider theater websites and word of mouth the "town." Anyway, I knew complete freedom would be too much, and when I said stuff like "This is my tender moment, you bitch," or, "You seem upset, sir—is it the $100? I'm on top of you, that's got to be worth at least $50," they started to rein me in. They still let me play around, within boundaries. Who knows? Maybe by the time this is published there will be an assault charge.

—Jackie Hoffman

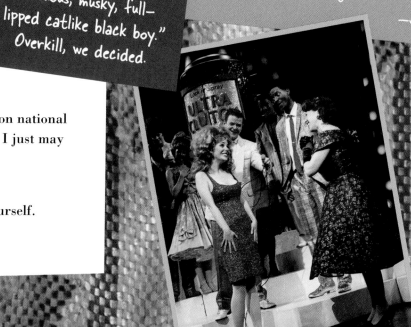

Everybody's Cinderella in this show.

WILBUR

That's my girl!

VELMA

Before I get completely sick, would somebody tell me this—if she came in through the front door . . . what the hell is in that can?

WILBUR

My masterpiece. Seaweed, would you give me a hand?

SEAWEED

Comin' right up, Mr. T.!
(SEAWEED climbs the giant hairspray can, ready to trigger it.)

WILBUR

This could be the largest novelty item ever erected. Fire!
(SEAWEED pushes the nozzle, and the hairspray can explodes in smoke and glitter to reveal EDNA dressed in finery.)

EDNA

So, what'd I miss? I've been stuck in that can since lunch. And I wouldn't rush right in there after me if I was you.

TRACY

Mama, we did it! We're on national TV.

EDNA

National television? America, I made this myself!

*YOU CAN'T STOP MY HAPPINESS
'CAUSE I LIKE THE WAY I AM
AND YOU JUST CAN'T STOP MY KNIFE AND FORK
WHEN I SEE A CHRISTMAS HAM
SO IF YOU DON'T LIKE THE WAY I LOOK
WELL, I JUST DON'T GIVE A DAMN!*

EDNA AND WILBUR	**BACKUP**
'CAUSE THE WORLD KEEPS SPINNING	*KEEPS SPINNING*
ROUND AND ROUND	*ROUND AND ROUND*
AND MY HEART'S KEEPING TIME	*KEEPING TIME*
TO THE SPEED OF SOUND	*TO THE SPEED OF SOUND*
I WAS LOST 'TIL I HEARD THE DRUMS	*'TIL I HEARD THE DRUMS*
THEN I FOUND MY WAY	*THEN I FOUND MY WAY*

Libretto

ALL
'CAUSE YOU CAN'T STOP THE BEAT
EVER SINCE THIS OLD WORLD BEGAN
A WOMAN FOUND OUT IF SHE SHOOK IT
SHE COULD SHAKE UP A MAN
AND SO I'M GONNA SHAKE AND SHIMMY IT
THE BEST THAT I CAN TODAY

'CAUSE YOU CAN'T STOP
THE MOTION OF THE OCEAN
OR THE SUN IN THE SKY
YOU CAN WONDER IF YOU WANNA
BUT I NEVER ASK WHY

AND IF YOU TRY TO HOLD ME DOWN
I'M GONNA SPIT IN YOUR EYE AND SAY
THAT YOU CAN'T STOP THE BEAT!

EDNA
Wilbur, be a dear and call for backup . . . NOW!
(MOTORMOUTH steps forward and removes her riot helmet.)

And her police outfit—to reveal a gold lamé dress!

WILBUR
Officer! Assistance please!

MOTORMOUTH
Step aside, Miss Buttercup, . . . it's time to wrap this mutha up!

	BACKUP
OH, OH, OH,	
YOU CAN'T STOP TODAY	*NO!*
AS IT COMES SPEEDING DOWN THE TRACK	*OO-OO-OO CHILD YES*
CHILD, YESTERDAY IS HIST'RY	*BE GONE*
AND IT'S NEVER COMING BACK	
	LOOK AHEAD
'CAUSE TOMORROW IS A BRAND NEW DAY	*'CAUSE TOMORROW . . .*
	. . . BRAND NEW DAY
AND IT DON'T KNOW WHITE FROM BLACK	
	YEAH!
'CAUSE THE WORLD KEEPS SPINNING	*KEEPS SPINNING*
ROUND AND ROUND	*ROUND AND ROUND*
AND MY HEART'S KEEPING TIME	*KEEPING TIME*
TO THE SPEED OF SOUND	*TO THE SPEED OF SOUND*

MOTORMOUTH (cont'd)
I WAS LOST 'TIL I HEARD THE DRUMS
THEN I FOUND MY WAY
'CAUSE YOU CAN'T STOP THE BEAT

BACKUP (cont'd)
'TIL I HEARD THE DRUMS
THEN I FOUND MY WAY

ALL
EVER SINCE WE FIRST SAW THE LIGHT
A MAN AND WOMAN LIKED TO SHAKE IT
ON A SATURDAY NIGHT
AND SO I'M GONNA SHAKE AND SHIMMY IT
WITH ALL MY MIGHT TODAY-AY-AY-AY

'CAUSE YOU CAN'T STOP
THE MOTION OF THE OCEAN
OR THE RAIN FROM ABOVE
THEY CAN TRY TO STOP THE PARADISE
WE'RE DREAMING OF
BUT THEY CANNOT STOP THE RHYTHM
OF TWO HEARTS IN LOVE TO STAY
'CAUSE YOU CAN'T STOP THE BEAT!

*(VELMA is by AMBER's side. They are defeated and confused until
the ENSEMBLE focuses on them . . .)*

AAH, AAH, AAH
AAH, AAH, AAH
AAH, AAH, AAH
COME ON YOU VON TUSSLES
GO ON AND SHAKE YOUR FANNY MUSCLES

VELMA & AMBER
WE CAN'T!

ALL
YES, YOU CAN!

VELMA & AMBER
NO, WE CAN'T!

ALL
YES, YOU CAN!

VELMA & AMBER
YES, WE CAN!!!

ALL
YOU CAN'T STOP THE BEAT

Even the villains are redeemed! Now that's the meaning of fiction!

VELMA & AMBER	**BACKUP**
EVER SINCE WE FIRST SAW THE SUN	OOH-OOH
IT SEEMS VON TUSSLE GIRLS ARE ALWAYS	
TRYIN' TO PLEASE SOMEONE	OOH-OOH
BUT NOW WE'RE GONNA	
SHAKE AND SHIMMY IT	OOH-OOH
AND HAVE SOME FUN TODAY	. . . TODAY

World Peace is briefly achieved.

ALL
'CAUSE YOU CAN'T STOP
THE MOTION OF THE OCEAN
OR THE RAIN FROM ABOVE
THEY CAN TRY TO STOP THE PARADISE
WE'RE DREAMING OF
BUT THEY CANNOT STOP THE RHYTHM
OF TWO HEARTS IN LOVE TO STAY
'CAUSE YOU CAN'T STOP THE BEAT!
YOU CAN'T STOP THE BEAT!!
YOU CAN'T STOP THE BEAT!!!

CURTAIN
END OF SHOW

opening

It's traditional on Broadway opening nights for the cast and creative team to exchange gifts—sort of like Christmas, Valentine's Day, and graduation all rolled into one. A lot of the *Hairspray* company had specially customized items made just for the occasion—including bathrobes, crystal vases, overnight bags, hand mirrors, and even, yes, engraved Zippo lighters.

Scott Wittman, Marc Shaiman and Suzanne Bartsch invite you to the "*Hairspray*" Opening Night AFTER PARTY 11 pm

GYPSY ROBE

Judine Richárd, a Dynamite

Receiving the Gypsy Robe on opening night, August 15, 2002, was, for me, the highlight not only of the evening but of my career. The robe is awarded to the musical ensemble member (or "gypsy") who has the most Broadway musical credits.

The ritual of the Gypsy Robe takes place onstage at opening night of every Broadway musical before the audience is admitted. The tradition began in 1950 when Bill Bradley, in the chorus of *Gentlemen Prefer Blondes*, persuaded a chorus girl to let him have her dressing gown. As a lark, he sent it to a friend on opening night of *Call Me Madam*, telling him it had been worn by all the Ziegfeld beauties. The friend added a rose from Ethel Merman's gown and sent it to a chorus member on the next opening night. It was then passed from show to show in a haphazard way and was often presented to a friend of the previous recipient or awarded to a chorus member based on popularity. Through the years the passing of the robe became a specific good-luck ceremony with official rules governing how the robe is to be presented, worn, and paraded onstage.

I'm so honored to be a part of the amazing group of "gypsies" who have received this award—Donna McKechnie, Chita Rivera, Cynthia Anrubia, and Gwen Verdon, to name a few.

167

THE CAST OF HAIRSPRAY

(in order of appearance)

OPENING NIGHT, AUGUST 15, 2002

Neil Simon Theatre

NEW YORK CITY

Tracy Turnblad.................... Marissa Jaret Winokur
Corny Collins........................ Clarke Thorell
Amber Von Tussle.................. Laura Bell Bundy
Brad................................... Peter Matthew Smith
Tammy................................ Hollie Howard
Fender................................ John Hill
Brenda............................... Jennifer Gambatese
Sketch............................... Adam Fleming
Shelley............................... Shoshana Bean
IQ..................................... Todd Michel Smith
Lou Ann.............................. Katharine Leonard
Link Larkin......................... Matthew Morrison
Prudy Pingleton.................... Jackie Hoffman
Edna Turnblad...................... Harvey Fierstein
Penny Pingleton.................... Kerry Butler
Velma Von Tussle.................. Linda Hart
Harriman F. Spritzer.............. Joel Vig
Wilbur Turnblad.................... Dick Latessa
Principal............................. Joel Vig
Seaweed Stubbs.................... Corey Reynolds
Duane................................ Eric Anthony
Gilbert............................... Eric Dysart
Lorraine............................. Danielle Lee Greaves
Thad.................................. Rashad Naylor
The Dynamites...................... Kamilah Martin, Judine Richárd, Shayna Steele
Mr. Pinky............................ Joel Vig
Gym Teacher........................ Jackie Hoffman
Little Inez........................... Danelle Eugenia Wilson
Motormouth Maybelle.............. Mary Bond Davis
Matron............................... Jackie Hoffman
Guard................................ Joel Vig
Denizens of Baltimore............. Eric Anthony, Shoshana Bean, Eric Dysart, Adam Fleming, Jennifer Gambatese, Danielle Lee Greaves, John Hill, Jackie Hoffman, Hollie Howard, Katharine Leonard, Kamilah Martin, Rashad Naylor, Judine Richárd, Peter Matthew Smith, Todd Michel Smith, Shayna Steele, Joel Vig
Swings............................... Joshua Bergasse, Greg Graham, Brooke Tansley

The show was cast by casting director extraordinaire Bernie Telsey. Two-thirds of the cast members remain from the show's very first read-through.